Bitcoin: Ever[ything You] Need To Know About This Cryptocurrency Craze

This books contains 4 Manuscripts:

Bitcoin: Beginners Bible

Cryptocurrency: Insider Secrets

Ethereum: Beginners Bible

Blockchain: Beginners Bible

By Stephen Satoshi

misuse of the information in question by the reader will render any resulting actions solely under their purview. There are no scenarios in which the publisher or the original author of this work can be in any fashion deemed liable for any hardship or damages that may befall them after undertaking information described herein.

Additionally, the information in the following pages is intended only for informational purposes and should thus be thought of as universal. As befitting its nature, it is presented without assurance regarding its prolonged validity or interim quality. Trademarks that are mentioned are done without written consent and can in no way be considered an endorsement from the trademark holder.

Financial Disclaimer:

I am not a financial advisor, this is not financial advice. This is not an investment guide nor investment advice. I am not recommending you buy any of the coins listed here. Any form of investment or trading is liable to lose you money.

There is no single "best" investment to be made, in cryptocurrencies or otherwise. Anyone telling you so is deceiving you.

There is no "surefire coin" - one again, anyone telling you so is deceiving you.

With many coins, especially the smaller ones, the market is liable to the spread of misinformation.

Never invest more than you are willing to lose. Cryptocurrency is not a get rich quick scheme.

Bitcoin Beginners Bible

Cryptocurrency Insider Secrets

Blockchain Beginners Bible

Bitcoin Beginners Bible: How You Can Profit from Trading and Investing in Bitcoin

By Stephen Satoshi

Introduction

This is normally the part with the drier than the Sahara Desert explanation of "you are going to learn blah blah..." that sends you straight to sleep.

Instead, I thought I'd do something a bit different and give you a quick overview of my own experience with Bitcoin.

I first heard of Bitcoin in 2011, during the first very first bubble, when I read a news report about this "internet money" thing that was worth $30 a piece. Did I invest then? I wish - I wasn't nearly informed enough. I honestly didn't understand how the technology worked or if Bitcoin was worth anything at all. After all, if a currency isn't backed by a government, how *can* it be worth anything? Oh to be that naive once again.

By the time I finally understood Bitcoin enough to be confident in buying some, the price had risen a hell of a lot more. But, now I believe in it as more than just a commodity to be traded or invested in. I believe in the technology at its core, and the potentially game changing ramifications for society at large. In that lies the true value of Bitcoin.

I wish I had a resource like this when I started out, something that explained the core concepts of Bitcoin and blockchain technology without reading like an astrophysics phD thesis. That's precisely why I wrote this book.

Happy reading, and I hope you not only make a lot of money with Bitcoin - I hope it has a truly profound and positive effect on your life.

Finally, if you enjoyed this book - I'd appreciate you taking just 2 minutes of your busy day to leave the book a review on Amazon.

Thanks,

Stephen

Bitcoin - A Brief History

Bitcoin is the first cryptocurrency that has lasted for more than 7 years and received any sort of mass adoption, but it took some time to get to this point. Before Bitcoin, there were a number of cryptocurrencies that reached some level of popularity. It all started back in 1980 when cryptographer David Chaum first developed the idea of a currency backed by a proof-of-work computer algorithm as opposed to a central bank. Chaum later went on to found DigiCash which had a briefly successful yet ultimately failed run at becoming the world's first mass adopted cryptocurrency. US based e-gold was possibly the most notable of the Pre-Bitcoin cryptocurrencies, although technologically it was significantly different from Bitcoin due to a centralized owner and non-fixed supply.

In August 2008, Neal Kin, Vladimir Oksman and Charles Bry filed a patent application for an encryption technology. The domain name Bitcoin.org was also registered in the same month using anonymousspeech.com which allowed for anonymous domain name registrations.

The big day came on October 31st 2008, Satoshi Nakamoto (a pseudonym with the true identity still unconfirmed) published a white paper named "Bitcoin: A Peer-to-Peer Electronic Cash System". The paper outlined various uses for the coin in addition to providing information about blockchain technology and how the coin would be mined using computer algorithms. The original white paper used Bitcoin as an example of a deflationary currency and one that governments or other central lenders could not artificially increase the money supply of, therefore devaluing a certain currency. The whitepaper also outlined issues with banks as trusted lenders, and how the blockchain's irreversible transaction design could reduce risk of fraud for merchants.

From January 2009 onwards, activists began mining the coin and the first Bitcoin blocks were created. Nakamoto and other cryptography enthusiasts began exchanging the coin for services with one another and in October 2009, the first official exchange rate was established for the coin of US$1 = 1,309.03 BTC. The original exchange rate was based on how much electricity it would cost to mine 1 Bitcoin.

The first real world transaction took place in May 2010 when enthusiast Laszlo Hanyecz bought two pizzas in Jacksonville, Florida for 10,000 BTC. Today 10,000BTC is worth over $40 million. A few months later in August, the first major Bitcoin hacking incident occured, the hacker exploited a vulnerability in the Bitcoin verification system and generated 184 billion Bitcoins. This led to the first major dip in the value of Bitcoin as a currency. This then led to government investigations of potential money laundering using Bitcoin. The early scares didn't last long though and In November 2010, Bitcoin reached a market capitalization of $1 million for the first time.

In January 2011, Bitcoin received a reasonable amount of mainstream coverage for the first time. Silk Road, an underground dark net website dealing in illicit goods such as illegal drugs and stolen credit cards was launched on the back of sending and receiving payments in Bitcoin. At its peak, it was estimated that up to 50% of Bitcoin transactions were ones that occured on Silk Road. The perceived anonymity of Bitcoin made it a favorite among Silk Road users. In February, Bitcoin reaches a market price of $1 for the first time and by July the coin had jumped to a value of $31.

2012 was somewhat of an uneventful year, although real world adoption continued with hosting platform Wordpress accepting the coin in November of that year. By March 2013, the market capitalization had reached $1 billion and Bitcoin exchange Coinbase reported over $1 million of Bitcoin transactions in a single month. In June, the DEA reported 11.02 Bitcoins as an asset during a drug seizure, the first time a government agency recognized Bitcoin as having inherent value. Drugs continued to make headlines as Silk Road owner Ross William Albricht was arrested in October, the FBI seized 26,000 Bitcoins from Silk Road servers during the arrest. Brighter news came the next month when the world's first Bitcoin ATM opened in Vancouver and China arrived on the scene when Chinese market activity overtook the US for the first time. By November of 2013, the price of 1 Bitcoin reached $1,000 for the first time.

December of 2013 came with China's central bank ruling that Bitcoin was not a currency and barred financial institution from accepting Bitcoins as a form of payment. In February 2014, Japanese based exchange Mt. Gox suspended Bitcoin withdrawals, citing technical issues. Within just a few weeks, the exchange had filed for bankruptcy amid claims of poor management and lack of security protocols. Roughly $740 million worth of Bitcoin, or 7% of the overall amount in circulation was lost in the incident. This issue led to the value of Bitcoin dropping 36% over the course of the month.

In June, TeraExchange LLC received approval from the U.S.Commodity Futures Trading Commission. This marked the first time that a U.S. agency approved a Bitcoin exchange. Computer manufacturer Dell began accepting Bitcoin as a means of payment at this time, the largest company to do so up to that point. AirBaltic also became the world's first airline to accept Bitcoin payments. In December, tech giant Microsoft began accepting payments in Bitcoin.

Coinbase, now one of the largest cryptocurrency exchange platforms received $75 million in a funding round, with the New York Stock Exchange being a minor investor. Further real world scaling continued and by August 2015, over 160,000 companies were accepting Bitcoin as a means of payment. December brought news of the potential identity of the notorious Satoshi Nakamoto figure. Wired magazine claimed the Australian Craig Wright was indeed Nakamoto. This led to a series of events that eventually resulted in a confirmation that Wright was indeed NOT Nakamoto.

July 2016 marked the second "halving day" in Bitcoin's history, where the reward for mining 1 block was halved to 12.5 Bitcoins per block. This was part of Bitcoin's original design to gradually decrease the supply of new coins available. The next halving is due to occur in 2020, with the total supply available to the market around the year 2140.

At the time of writing, Bitcoin trades for around $4,000 per coin on exchanges.

Basics of Blockchain Technology

While we could spend an entire book on blockchain and the technology behind it alone, it is important to understand the fundamentals if you're planning to invest in Bitcoin, or any other cryptocurrency.

Blockchain is a decentralized ledger, meaning it is a record that is publicly accessible and can be verified by anyone. This is important for any non-tangible good as the unlike tangible goods like socks or candy, we need a record of a transaction happening in case something goes wrong. For example, we need proof that Steve paid John for the pair of socks that John sold him. The blockchain will have a record of a transaction from Steve's account to John's account, and no one else's.

Previously, we would have the use a third party, like a bank, to verify the transaction did indeed take place. The bank would then take their % of the total transaction. As the bank information is not publicly accessible, we would also have to trust that the bank did their job. By using blockchain technology, we have a 100% infallible record of the transaction taking place, and anyone can see this. There's also no need to pay a large additional fee to a middleman. The only fee involved is the cost of running the blockchain itself.

If we only use blockchain for financial purposes, this is extremely useful in countries that do not have a trustworthy banking sector. Each transaction is recorded as a block, with a date and timestamp. These blocks cannot be altered without everyone seeing. The problem this solves is known as the "double-spending problem", where digital assets (like cryptocurrency) have the potential to be spent more than once. What the blockchain allows us to do is see that Steve has already used his money to pay John, so he can't then use that same money to try and pay Sally. The blockchain creates trust among all parties, and trust is paramount when dealing with monetary transactions.

Blockchain's uses are not strictly financial. We can also use the technology to store other information that we would need in a publicly available, transparent form. This ranges from anything like voting records in an election, to a self-executing contract between two parties that fulfills when both parties have completed their obligations. Blockchain eliminates the need for a middleman, or independent auditor in these situation, as the technology itself acts both as an auditor, and as an independent. In theory, the technology has the power to replace accountants, lawyers and much of the financial services industry. Before we get ahead of ourselves though, much of the non-financial uses of blockchain technology are still strictly, in theory.

How does Bitcoin Work?

Bitcoin functions as a digital currency, by following the same three rules that traditional, or fiat currencies follow.

1. They need to be difficult to produce (cash) or find (gold or other precious metals)

2. They need have a limited supply

3. They need to be recognized by other humans as having value

When we examine Bitcoin, it ticks the boxes of all three of these characteristics:

1. Bitcoin uses complex computer algorithms in its production which take a lot of computational power and proof-of-work, so it cannot be replicated easily or at a discount

2. There are a finite supply of Bitcoins - 21 Million to be exact. As of 2015, roughly 2/3 of this number had been mined

3. There are hundreds of Bitcoin exchanges and Bitcoin is accepted as payment everywhere from Subway to OKCupid

Bitcoin miners have incentive to mine as they receive Bitcoin as a reward for their computer's endeavors. Bitcoin was designed to be a deflationary currency, so unlike fiat currencies, the supply of money is fixed. This, combined with the decentralization principle ensure that no single person or government can simply create additional coins once the supply is mined. Once all the coins are mined, the value of the currency will in theory, continue to rise.

Bitcoin transactions are recorded on a digital ledger (or record) known as the blockchain. The core concept that upholds Bitcoin's usefulness is decentralization. With decentralization, the blockchain is not owned by one single person or entity. In fact, everyone has access to it. Therefore transactions are publicly broadcasted across the network, which ensures that both parties have upheld their end of the agreement. The code is open source (like Linux or Android Operating Systems) so anyone can view it, this ensures transparency among all parties.

Decentralization allows the blockchain to be secured by multiple points of entry and backed up by multiple points of failure. This is turn prevents incidents like hacking or theft. For example, if someone offers you 1 Bitcoin, you can check the blockchain records to make sure that Bitcoin is valid and hasn't already been spent. This system means we do not need third parties to validate the transactions. The only transactions costs come from the electricity or mining power needed to run the blockchain itself.

This has tremendous real world application, from allowing cheaper international payments (since Bitcoin has no nationality) to lowering the overall price of certain goods.

Bitcoin as a Store of Wealth

Bitcoin's status as a deflationary currency makes it incredibly useful in times where fiat currency is undergoing gross levels of inflation. Like gold has been traditionally used in times of economic hardship, Bitcoin has the potential to do the same. To be used as a store of value or wealth, Bitcoin has a fulfill a few criteria.

1. It has to not be perishable
2. It has to not depreciate over time

The second criteria is somewhat debatable, as critics argue that Bitcoin could depreciate due to better technology surpassing it. However, Bitcoin has now reached a certain market point where the idea itself has an intrinsic value, like say email or Facebook. Email isn't particularly useful if you're the only one with an address to send mail to, but the more people use the technology, the easier, and more valuable it is.

Venezuela is currently undergoing the worst cash crisis of the decade. Inflation has reached a level where people's money is nigh-on worthless against the US dollar, and much of the country cannot afford basic necessities. That is, except for those who hold Bitcoins, whose value against the US dollar continues to increase.

China is doing the same thing, albeit for different reasons. Traditional investments in Chinese assets have returned less than previous years due to the government's devaluation of the Yuan. Converting money to gold and silver is heavily regulated and often incurs large transaction costs. Bitcoin does not suffer from any of these issues, and often is the only alternative for those who are looking to secure their wealth in both the short and long term.

Gold has long been the traditional backup plan, or "hedge" against uncertain financial markets. In times of war, or financial crisis, gold prices tend to rise when financial markets are falling. However, in recent times this has not been the case. At the time of writing, gold's 12 month performance is stagnant, whereas Bitcoin has risen by nearly 1000%. Growing tensions in North Korea are just one factor that has spurned Bitcoin's growth in times of uncertainty. Tensions in the region have led to increased buys from the Chinese, Japanese and South Korean markets.

8 Common Bitcoin Myths Debunked

Like all technological innovations, there are a number of points that uninformed players do not understand. As such, misinformation spreads which causes fear, uncertainty and doubt - which only hurts the technology going forward.

1.   Bitcoin is illegal

Let's deal with the big one off the bat shall we? Just because a currency is not backed by a government, does not make it illegal. For you, the user, by operating as a virtual currency, Bitcoin is legal, so long as you are using it for legal means.

2. Miners or developers can change the amount of Bitcoins available to benefit themselves

The way the Bitcoin algorithm works ensures there are no shortcuts in obtaining one. If a counterfeit Bitcoin does not satisfy all the conditions required, any transactions made using it will be rejected. This is similar to how banks reject counterfeit bank notes.

3. Bitcoin isn't worth anything because it isn't backed by a central government

With all currencies, they are only worth what someone is willing to exchange for them. In the same way that gold or US dollars have no inherent value, Bitcoin is just a means of exchange.

4. Bitcoin's main use is for criminals and the government will shut it down

Yes, at one time a significant % of Bitcoin usage was used for illegal activity. Much of this activity was facilitated on the underground black market website Silk Road. However, this is no longer the case. Bitcoin is now accepted by over 160,000 merchants worldwide and adoption continues to grow. The technological uses like minimized transactions fees have far more use for large financial institutions than they do for some basement dwelling 20 year trying to buy LSD from a guy in another country. It's worth noting that fiat currencies are also used for criminal activity.

This one also relies on the myth that Bitcoin is completely anonymous. Yes, there are no named Bitcoin accounts, but each Bitcoin address is unique and every transaction is recorded on a public ledger (the blockchain). Therefore with a little legwork, it is possible to determine who is behind a Bitcoin transaction.

As far as a potential government shutdown does, that's a little trickier. Governments do have the power to make life difficult for citizens dealing strictly in Bitcoin, but this difficulty only goes as far as taxation on Bitcoin.

5. **21 Million Bitcoins is too small of a total number for effective daily use**

Where this one falls short is that it fails to compute that Bitcoin is divisible to eight decimal places. 0.00000001 BTC is actually the smallest unit available, this is also known as 1 Satoshi. There are really 2,099,999,997,690,000 (just over 2 quadrillion) maximum possible units or Satoshi in the Bitcoin system. When 1 Bitcoin becomes too large for day-to-day transactions, we will simply move on to smaller units for convenience, similar to how we use pennies now for small transactions.

6.   Hackers can simply steal all the Bitcoins

It's important to differentiate between exchanges or websites being hacked, and the blockchain itself being hacked. Exchange hacks exploit security weaknesses of private companies, whereas the blockchain is not centralized so there is no single weakness for hackers to exploit. The same argument can be applied to the US dollar, just because a store is robbed does not mean the US dollar as a currency has been stolen from the source. That said, you should take appropriate security precautions when storing your Bitcoin such as creating a safe, offline wallet.

7.   Bitcoin is a pyramid scheme/Ponzi scheme

My personal favorite. Pyramid schemes are a zero sum game. The founders and early adopters profit from the money put into the scheme by late adopters. With Bitcoin everyone can profit, no matter when they first made their initial investment. The other illusion here is that there is one central founder of Bitcoin. Bitcoin is decentralized and there is no "CEO" or person at the top of the pyramid.

8. Bitcoin is dead/There is no point investing in Bitcoin now

I have witnessed at least 20 "Bitcoin deaths" in the past 5 years alone. From hacking incidents to Silk Road Founder Ross William Albricht's arrest, detractors have used these as fuel for Bitcoin's obtituary. The numbers don't lie though, and Bitcoin is in a stronger position than ever both in terms of market capitalization and real world adoption.

As early as 2012, you can find commentators saying it was "too late" to invest in Bitcoin. Yet, real world adoption continues to grow, and the price keeps on rising. Is that to say there won't be issues in the future? I'm sure there will be. However, if Bitcoin transactions keep increasing, the currency shows no signs of slowing down any time soon.

Latest Bitcoin Innovations: SegWit, Lightning Network

The number one technical issue Bitcoin faces in its lifetime is the issue of scalability. Or in real world terms, Bitcoin's ability to handle a growing number of transactions. Currently, each Block on the Bitcoin network is 1MB, representing 10 minutes per transaction, which increases during periods of heavy use. This is beneficial for banks and large financial institutions as 10 minutes is a far quicker processing time than that of say SWIFT or other payment networks. However, in terms of smaller businesses, like say a coffee shop, 10 minutes is an incredibly long and non-practical payment time.

For years, there has been a constant disagreement about the best way to upgrade Bitcoin's block sizes. The longer these arguments continue, the slower any proposed solutions are developed. There are two main camps, those who favor a hard fork, which loosens up the rules of the protocol and those who favor a soft fork, which tightens the rules of the current protocol.

Without going into advanced technical details, users who favor a soft fork are currently proposing a solution known as Segregated Witness or SegWit. The crux of SegWit is that the signature (or *witness)* of a transaction can be kept on a separate block from the transaction itself, this frees up block space for additional transactions. The witness data is encrypted and cannot be modified, so there is no ability to change the information of the payment sender. This has great real world usage in terms of lowering the ability to hack a transaction.

As with any potential change, there is a certain amount of unpredictability involved. In practical terms, SegWit activation will affect the price of Bitcoin one way or another in the short term, however at the time of writing, SegWit has only been activated for less than 72 hours, and the price has held stable thus far.

The activation of SegWit could well pave way for the lightning network, a technology that will enable instant Bitcoin transactions. Instant transactions as previously stated, will help micro and nano transactions immensely, and allow small businesses to utilize the benefits of accepting payments in Bitcoin at point of sale terminals. This will be especially useful in countries with low-value fiat currencies. One current example of this is Venezuela, where the Venezuelan Bolivar has lost around 90% of its value against the US dollar in under a year. Bitcoin transactions are helping a small, but significant portion of Venezuelan public hold value in the money they do have.

So what is Bitcoin Cash then?

Bitcoin Cash (BCH or BCC on exchanges) is a spin-off cryptocurrency that was the result of the August 1st hard fork by a small, yet significant proportion of the Bitcoin mining community. The fork involves increased block sizes and faster transaction times which in turn will lead to lower transaction fees. The blocksize has increased to 8MB, from the original 1MB that Bitcoin uses. This fork was designed to solve the scalability problems that Bitcoin currently faces.

So if Bitcoin Cash is technologically superior to Bitcoin, why don't I invest in that instead?

It's a tough question to answer because quite frankly, these are still very early days. At the time of writing the fork is only 1 month old and Bitcoin Cash has had high price fluctuations. Liquidity is much lower than Bitcoin (meaning it is difficult to sell large amounts) and real world adoption effects remain to be determined. If you're a new investor, Bitcoin Cash is certainly something to be monitored. However, the network effects of Bitcoin are still too strong to ignore, and it is still very much the number one cryptocurrency.

In terms of market price, the Bitcoin Cash split on August 1st initially led to a fall in the price of Bitcoin, before it once again rose to an all-time-high in late August. Bitcoin Cash value initially plummeted before a boom and then a reset to its current price of around $550.

If you purchased Bitcoin after August 1st, Bitcoin Cash should be treated as a completely separate currency. Any Bitcoin transaction will not be replicated in Bitcoin Cash or vice versa. If you wish to purchase Bitcoin, look for the symbol BTC on exchanges. If you purchased Bitcoin before August 1st you may well be able to receive the same amount in Bitcoin Cash - providing you held it in a wallet that was not linked to any exchange.

For miners, or those interested in mining, at the time of writing Bitcoin Cash offers greater mining rewards when compared to Bitcoin, due to a decreased difficulty in its proof-of-work algorithm.

How to Buy Bitcoin

Gone are the days when buying Bitcoin was a time consuming and somewhat uncomfortable endeavor. Nowadays buying Bitcoin is a similar process to exchanging currency when you go on vacation.

There are two ways to buy Bitcoin, the first is to use fiat currency (USD, EUR, GBP etc.) to purchase cryptocurrency via an exchange. These exchanges function the same way as regular foreign currency exchanges do. The prices fluctuate on a daily basis, and like regular currency exchange markets - they are open 24/7. These exchanges make their money from charging a small fee for each transaction.

Some charge both buyers and sellers, some only charge a fee for buying. For security reasons, most of these exchanges will require you to verify your ID before allowing you to purchase cryptocurrency.

It is also important to note the type of payments each exchange supports. Some allow for debit/credit card payments whereas other only accept PayPal or bank wire transfers. Below are the three biggest and reputable currency exchanges for purchasing Bitcoin, Ethereum and other altcoins with fiat currency like US dollars, Euros or British Pounds.

Coinbase

Currently largest currency exchange in the world, Coinbase allows users to buy, sell and store cryptocurrency. Coinbase is undoubtedly the most beginner friendly exchange for anyone looking to get involved in the cryptocurrency market. They currently allow trading of Bitcoin, as well as, Ethereum and

LiteCoin using fiat currency as a base. Known for their stellar security procedures and insurance policies regarding stored currency. The exchange also has a fully functioning iPhone and Android app for buying and selling on the go, very useful if you are looking to trade.

Once you are signed up and complete the identity verification procedures you can buy Bitcoin with your credit or debit card instantly.

If you sign up for Coinbase using this link, you will receive $10 worth of free Bitcoin after your first purchase of more than $100 worth of cryptocurrency.

http://bit.ly/10dollarbtc

Kraken

Based in Canada, and currently the largest exchange in terms of volume of buys in Euros, Kraken has the advantage of more coin support (they also allow the purchase of Monero, Ethereum Classic and Dogecoin) than Coinbase. It allows margin trading, which while beyond the scope of a beginner, will be of interest to more experienced traders

For other altcoins, you will need access to an exchange that facilitates cryptocurrency to cryptocurrency trading. The best one of these is Poloniex.

Poloniex

With more than 100 different cryptocurrencies available and data analysis for advanced traders, Poloniex is the most comprehensive exchange on the market. Low trading fees are another plus, this is a great place to trade your Bitcoin into other cryptocurrencies. If you have never purchased Bitcoin before, you will no be able to do so as Poloniex does not allow fiat currency deposits. Therefore, you will have to make your initial Bitcoin purchases on Coinbase or Kraken.

Buying Locally

The second way to buy Bitcoins in exchange for fiat currency is to locally purchase them in person. The advantage of this is that you may be able to get a marginally better price than by using an exchange. The other advantage is that users living in countries that don't have easy access to online exchanges can still buy coins in person. All transactions are protected by Escrow to prevent either party being scammed.

Website http://localbitcoins.com is the current market leader for local bitcoin transactions with sellers in over 15,000 cities around the world.

How To Safely Store Your Bitcoin

Congratulations on purchasing your first Bitcoins! Now that you've bought your Bitcoin, you'll need to keep it secure. You can do this by transferring it off the exchange and into what is known as a Bitcoin wallet. The name wallet implies that you can do all the same things you can with a regular wallet. You can see how much Bitcoin you have, and use it to spend your Bitcoin. An important distinction to make is that because Bitcoin is decentralized and stored on the Blockchain, these wallets do not "store" your Bitcoin per say.

While exchanges like Coinbase do provide you with your own wallet, unless you are day-trading, it's advisable to remove your coins from the exchange in order to prevent against issues like hacking - which unfortunately does happen

In 2011, Tokyo based Bitcoin exchange Mt. Gox suffered losses of over $27.2 million and 80,000 users lost a total of over $460 million worth of Bitcoin after the exchange was hacked. Mt. Gox wasn't some fly by night operation either, in fact at the time it was the largest cryptocurrency exchange on Earth. Yet poor security protocols and mismanagement allowed the attacks to occur. The company eventually filed for bankruptcy amid allegations of fraud, and much of the userbase's stolen coins have not been recovered to this day. This is why it's paramount that if you want to hold your coins for the long-term, you store them safely.

The understand wallets, we must first understand just how they work. Bitcoin transactions need both a private key (from the sender) and a public key (from the receiver) in order to process correctly on the blockchain.

A public key is a series of between 26 and 35 alphanumeric characters e.g. 1Co5CmEZNz35Am59EcFhKGRdNfLrzppGkJ

If you can this address to someone, they can send funds to your wallet. It is perfectly safe for you to give your public key, also known as your wallet address, to anyone, as they can only deposit into your account with this information. In 2013, a college student received 22 Bitcoins (then worth around $24,000) by holding up a sign with his public key in the form of a QR code on an edition of ESPN's College Gameday.

Your private key on the other hand should be held by you, and you alone. **Never give your private key to anyone.**

There are numerous types of wallets you can use, here is a breakdown of each one.

Desktop Wallets

A desktop wallet are a convenient medium between moving your Bitcoins off an exchange, while not having to carry around additional information like with a paper or hardware wallet. You can think of these like a Bitcoin bank account on your computer. Most desktop wallets will encrypt your private keys for you to add an extra layer of security. Here is a run-down of some of the more popular desktop Bitcoin wallets. All the wallets listed below are free, you should never pay for a desktop wallet.

Electrum - https://electrum.org

While it's design may not win any awards, Electrum does the job it's supposed to. The code is open source, which means there's a much lower possibility of the development team slipping in something malicious.

Electrum allows you to store and spend your Bitcoins with relative ease. It has the advantage of storing your private keys offline, and to go online in "watching only" mode, so if your computer gets hacked during the process, hackers won't be able to spend any coins. It also has support for various hardware wallets.

Exodus - https://www.exodus.io/

Unlike Electrum, Exodus is not open source. However, Exodus does have the advantage of being capable of storing other coins like Ethereum, Litecoin and Dogecoin in addition to Bitcoin. The interface is also more user-friendly than Electrum.

It should be noted, that as desktop wallets require your computer to be connected to the internet, they can never be 100% secure.

CoPay - https://copay.io

CoPay operates on both desktop and mobile platforms, so it's great if you're looking to spend or receive Bitcoins on the go. It requires multiple signatures (ways of account verification) to spend coins, which is an added security feature. There's a multiple user option as well, which is useful for groups and families. The software's code being open source is always a plus.

Paper Wallets

Paper wallets are simply notes of your private key that are written down on paper. They will often feature QR codes so the sender can quickly scan them to send cryptocurrency.

Pros:

- Cheap

- Your private keys are not stored digitally, and are therefore not subject to cyber-attacks or hardware failures.

Cons:

- Loss of paper due to human error

- Paper is fragile and can degrade quickly in certain environments

- Not easy to spend cryptocurrency quickly if necessary - not useful for everyday transactions

You can use sites like bitaddress.org to create non-secure paper wallets online. These are known as non-secure as you have to be connected to the internet in order to use them. If the site is hacked, then hackers can access information regarding all private keys that have ever been created.

Step by Step Guide on How to Create a 100% Secure Paper Wallet

Required Material:

- **Offline download of bitaddress -** http://bit.ly/offlinebitaddress

- **Lili Live USB -** http://www.linuxliveusb.com/en/download

- **Ubuntu Operating System -** http://www.ubuntu.com/download/desktop

- **USB Flash Drive -** either a brand new or one you are willing to format the existing data from

- **A printer**

Installing Ubuntu on your flash drive

1. Download the above programs

2. Open LiLi and insert your USB flash drive into your computer

3. In Lili choose a source - select "ISO/IMG/Zip" option

4. In Lili Options - select "Format the key in FAT32"

5. Unzip the offline bitaddress file and copy it into your flash drive

Then disconnect your computer from the internet - this is so there is no way anyone can access your computer while you are creating a private key.

Booting Ubuntu from your flash drive

Reboot your computer, and press F12 before windows or OSX loads. Select USB HDD from the boot menu. Then run the Ubuntu operating system from your flash drive. After it has loaded, click on "Try Ubuntu"

Once Ubuntu has loaded, click on system settings then printers and add your printer. Print out 1 page to test it has connected.

Creating your wallet

6. Click on the Firefox icon on Ubuntu and open the private browsing window

7. Type in the following in the address bar: <u>file:///cdrom/bitaddress.org-master/</u>

8. Click on "BitAddress.org.html"

9. Move your cursor around until the timer reaches 0 (this is to ensure that you are a real person)

10. Choose Paper Wallet

11. Follow the steps to print out your paper wallet

12. Deposit BTC using the public address on the left hand side of the wallet (represented by a QR code)

Additional Recommendations

It is recommended you store your paper wallet in a sealed plastic bag to protect against water or damp conditions. Make multiple copies for extra security and if you are holding cryptocurrency for the long-term, store the paper inside a safe.

Hardware Wallets

Hardware wallets refer to physical storage items that contain your private key. The most common form of these are encrypted USB sticks. These are similar to ones you can make yourself, except someone else has already set up the security protocols for you. This is ideal for those who are non-tech savvy. Many of them also have built-in backup software in case you lose your keys.

These wallets use two factor authentication or 2FA to ensure that only the wallet owner can access the data. For example, one factor is the physical USB stick plugged into your computer, and the other would be a 4 digit pin code - much like how you use a debit card to withdraw money from an ATM.

Pros:

- Near impossible to hack - as of the time of writing, there have been ZERO instances of hacked hardware wallets

- Even if your computer is infected with a virus or malware, the wallet cannot be accessed due to 2FA

- The private key never leaves your device or transfers to a computer, so once again, malware or infected computers are not an issue

- Can be carried with you easily if you need to spend your cryptocurrency

- Transactions are easier than with paper wallets

- Can store multiple addresses on one device - good if you plan on having multiple Bitcoin accounts

- For the gadget lovers among you - they look a lot cooler than a folded piece of paper

Cons:

- More expensive than paper wallets - starting at around $60

- Susceptible to hardware damage, degradation and changes in technology

- Different wallets support different cryptocurrencies

- Trusting the provider to deliver an unused wallet. Using a second hand wallet is a big security breach. Only purchase hardware wallets from official sources.

The most popular of these are the Trezor and Ledger wallets. Both of these provide an easy to use experience in addition to being a portable and secure way to store your Bitcoin.

How to Trade Bitcoin

While you may want to hold Bitcoin for the long term, you may also wish to trade them for other cryptocurrencies or fiat currency. This is the fastest way to make money with Bitcoin, but also the riskiest. To trade for fiat currency, you can simply sell them at the current exchange rate on the same exchange you bought them at, like Coinbase or Kraken.

If you want to trade them for other cryptocurrencies however, it's best to move them to Poloniex or another large exchange like Bittrex. Once on here you will see the exchange rate between Bitcoin and other currencies. It should be noted that this may differ from the exchange rate for the cryptocurrency to fiat pairing. For example, the exchange rate for BTC to Litecoin (LTC) may differ from the rate for BTC/USD and LTC/USD. Fees are usually low for crypto-to-crypto trades, the maximum fee on Poloniex for example is 0.25%.

Another element you should examine is the liquidity for certain pairings. For example, you don't want a trade to be delayed because someone on the exchange is not selling the volume of the coin you are buying. To check liquidity of certain coin pairings go to http://coinmarketcap.com

These exchanges also along you to view the historical price charts for the various pairings as well as the liquidity (ease of making a trade) for each market.

As with any speculative market, trading Bitcoin is risky and you are liable to lose money. This is especially true if you trade on emotion, and not rationality. It is advisable to proceed with caution and do your homework before you do any trading for real. You can practice with virtual money (known as paper trading) on sites like https://www.whaleclub.co/

Needless to say though, you will make mistakes at first.
You'll learn from these mistakes, but it's important
that you make them with money you can afford to
lose.

If you are going to trade, take intermediate profits for
yourself. This way any gains you have made are in your
bank account, and not just on paper. Dollar cost
averaging also applies to trading in addition to
investing.

What Determines the Price of Bitcoin?

If you're going to invest in Bitcoin, or any cryptocurrency for that matter, it's important to understand the market factors that drive the price one way or another. There are a number of these, which often interact with one another, but for simplicity purposes, we will examine them one by one.

China

No country has more of an effect on the price of Bitcoin than China. More fiat to Bitcoin trades from China than any other country, and some of the largest exchanges in the world are based there. Approximately 70% of the world's Bitcoin trades occur in the Chinese market.

Good news from China equals good news for the market in general. A December 2013 announcement from the People's Bank of China decreeing that Bitcoin was not a currency tanked the market by 35% in under an hour. Conversely, news of Bitcoin being adopted by Chinese business often leads to the Bitcoin price rising.

One major factor that makes China such a driving force in the Bitcoin market is the Chinese government's strict financial regulation of assets held in Chinese Yuan. Both wealthy and middle class Chinese citizens are looking for a way to secure their financial future without tying it to the value of the Yuan, which has been devalued in recent years. Bitcoin represents the perfect way for them to do this. Further Yuan devaluation will only lead to increased Bitcoin growth in the future.

Russia

Like China, Russia is also suffering from issues with its fiat currency, the ruble. The ruble has continued to fall against the US dollar year-on-year for the past 3 years. As it does so, Russians like to protect their wealth by moving their rubles into Bitcoin.

Adoption is Russia is also a major player in Bitcoin short-term price movements. An announcement in May 2017 that Ulmart, the largest online retailer in Russia, would begin accepting Bitcoin payments, took the market to a then all time high of $1800.

Government Regulation

Government support for Bitcoin will also play a part in the price of it as a commodity. Although Bitcoin is not tied to any one nation, for mass adoption to occur - it needs the support of government. The main contention for governments right now is Bitcoin's perceived "complete anonymity" and how it relates to crime, especially tax evasion. Once measures are in place to eliminate the anonymity element (regardless of your moral standpoint on this), government support will rise, and so will the price of Bitcoin.

Conversely, any time there is news of a government crackdown on Bitcoin either as a digital currency, or on a technology level - the price decreases

Technological Innovation

Advances in the Bitcoin network are vital if it is to continue increasing in value. As previously mentioned, new developments like SegWit and the lighting network, which will ease scalability issues, are important in the development of the coin on a technological front.

The coin's ability to handle micropayments (transactions of small monetary value) is one key area that was have a big effect on the future value. Currently the effectiveness of the system for micropayments is limited by the 1MB block size, which leads to minimum transaction amounts and delays in payment processing if you send too many transactions too quickly. With the implementation of lightning network, the team hopes to ease these issues and further increase Bitcoin's real world viability.

Mass Media

Despite what we'd like to believe, the vast majority of society still get their news from just 1 or 2 sources. To put it bluntly, the mainstream media doesn't understand Bitcoin one iota. Due to the lack of proper cryptocurrency or crypto asset journalists working for major outlets, they would rather give airtime to good soundbites like "Bitcoin could reach $100,000 within 5 years" or inversely "Bitcoin is the biggest bubble since the dotcom craze" than examine it at a technological level, or focus on any innovations that have been made. Positive news for Bitcoin in the media leads to new investors, and negative news leads to a decrease in price.

The other side of this is that some Bitcoin commentators have already made up their mind without even examining the technology. If you see an article in 2017 talking about Bitcoin as a front for "drug dealing" or "money laundering", then you can safely disregard it.

For your own personal news source, I recommend dedicated sites like http://coindesk.com for legitimate, non-biased or overhyped news regarding Bitcoin and cryptocurrency.

Funding for Blockchain Companies

As blockchain companies continue to receive more funding and investment, the currency receives more legitimization. Many blockchain related startups now accept investments in Bitcoin and other cryptocurrencies like Ethereum.

The Middle Class Investor

An often overlooked factor. While Bitcoin may be increasing in popularity among younger investors and some larger institutions, it is still very much off the radar of the American middle class. In other words think about Tom, aged 55, from Maryland. He's married and has a low 6 figure income from his upper management job. His portfolio currently consists mainly of blue chip stocks and low-cost index funds. He's not trying to hit any home runs, he's just trying to shore up his retirement assets. Once Bitcoin cements its reputation as a form of "digital gold" and more of a solid long-term investment rather than the speculative play thing it is seen as by some major institutions, it's value will continue to rise. In other words, we need more people like Tom as our target Bitcoin buyer for the value to continue increasing.

Technical Analysis

It should be noted that traditional technical analysis or chart analysis like one would do on stocks is tough, as the cryptocurrency market is a) only 8 years old so lacks comprehensive data and b) unlike anything we've ever seen before. However, charting does have its place in the Bitcoin universe and I would recommend you study stock technical analysis books if you are planning to trade Bitcoin on a serious level, with candlestick charting being the most useful for the cryptocurrency market.

Mass Adoption

As more merchants accept Bitcoin as a means of payment, the more it legitimizes the currency. Bitcoin's scalability issues will be the main determinant of this. Adoption shows no sign of slowing down and the total number of businesses accepting the currency continues to grow. If corporate giants such as Amazon and Apple began to accept Bitcoin payments, then the price is likely to increase once again.

Bitcoin for Business: How Your Business can Benefit from Accepting Bitcoin Payments

If you're not a small business owner, you can skip this section, but if you are, I advise you to pay close attention.

First and foremost, accepting Bitcoin payments can save you money.

While traditional credit card payment processing are around 2-3%. Using Bitcoin payment platforms such as BitPay can reduce these fees to around 1%. Even a small percentage change like this can represent big savings in the long run. If you're an internet seller tired of bank's charging you extortionate fees for currency conversions, or simply want to make your product or service accessible worldwide - Bitcoin may be your solution. Bitcoin doesn't discriminate across borders, and payments from any countries are subject to the same transaction costs.

There are millions of Bitcoin users looking for places to spend their coins, adding your business to the equation can only be good for the network as a whole. Bitcoin users are also an enthusiastic bunch, and enjoy supporting businesses that accept it. Cryptocurrency as a whole is a growing market, and making your business an early adopter is a chance to become a player in your industry via increased brand awareness.

There's also protection against chargeback fraud. As Bitcoin payments are irreversible, you, the merchant is no longer responsible for the costs of fraud.

For non-profits, Bitcoin donations have soared year-on-year since its inception. The Jamaican Bobsled team funded their trip to the 2014 Winter Olympics entirely from cryptocurrency donations. There's also the benefits of customers seeing the total donation amount and where it is spent in a sector where transparency is king.

If you're worried about the fluctuation of Bitcoin's value, then services like BitPay have you covered with daily bank transfers in your local currency.

Can I Still Make Money with Bitcoin in 2017?

Short answer: Yes

Long answer: Bitcoin continues to grow, both as a digital asset and as a currency with real world applications. Increased globalization and the need to transfer money across borders will only lead to a rise in adoption of Bitcoin. The amount of cross border money transfers continues to grow year-on-year and now represent almost 1% of the world's GDP. Bitcoin's total market cap now stands at $71 billion, more than the GDP of countries like Costa Rica and Bulgaria.

The near (but not total) anonymous element of Bitcoin is another factor that continues to drive growth. This is particularly important in countries where government's heavily regulate the fiat currency like China.

Bitcoin has now become a brand in and of itself. The currency is synonymous with a digital store of value. This is something that no other cryptocurrency can touch. Think of it like buying a property. Would you rather buy one in a "name brand" city like London or New York, where the demand for properties like yours will always be high, regardless of the general state of the market. Or one for the same price in say Oklahoma City where you may be able to buy a bigger house - but will you be able to sell during a market downturn?

Whether you want to use Bitcoin as a tool for trading, exchanging for other cryptocurrencies or as a long term store of value, there has never been a better time to invest in cryptocurrency than 2017. It's also never been easier to invest with sites like Coinbase and Kraken.

Just remember though, everyone feels like a genius or ahead of the curve when the market is going up. There will be down periods, and it's important to manage your risk correctly so that you can ride out the bad times and continue to profit during the good ones. Remember this - even the best in the business get it wrong sometimes

The Bitcoin Investing Mindset and How to Minimize Your Risk

In a market as volatile as cryptocurrency, it's important to minimize your risk as much as possible. With potential market changes of 10% on a daily basis, it's important for your portfolio, as well as, your peace of mind.

First off, never invest more than you can afford to lose. It may be tempting to try and hit a home run, but in doing so you will cause yourself sleepless nights and anxiety ridden days.

Secondly, unless you are day trading, don't check crypto price charts every few hours. Doing so will only give additional anxiety. The price is liable is swing by large percentage margins on a daily basis, that's just the way of the Bitcoin market, just remember that so far, over the long run, the price has continued to increase.

Dollar Cost Averaging

One of the best ways to minimize your risk in a volatile market is to use what is known as 'dollar cost averaging'. This simply means dividing up your total planned investment and buying Bitcoin at regular intervals instead of all at once.

With dollar cost averaging, you are simply buying less of an asset (in this case, Bitcoin) when the price is high, and more when the price is low. Your total exposure is less because you are only exposed to part of any decline in the market, as opposed to all of it with a lump sum investment. Your average cost per coin is therefore likely to be lower.

Let's use an example, both Alan and John have $1200 to invest in Bitcoin at the start of 2015. Alan decides to invest all $1200 on January 1st, John on the other hand is going to use dollar cost averaging. He will invest $100 on the 1st of each month, for a total of $1200. The prices used in this example are the actual Bitcoin trading prices as of those dates.

January 1st 2015 - $305.32

February 1st 2015 - $237.18

March 1st 2015 - $263.57

April 1st 2015 - $255.23

May 1st 2015 - $226.45

June 1st 2015 - $233.44

July 1st 2015 - $260.73

August 1st 2015 -$283.04

September 1st 2015 - $229.00

October 1st 2015 - $240.10

November 1st 2015 - $325.28

December 1st 2015 - $375.95

Alan's total investment in BTC = 3.93 (1200/305.32)

John's total investment in BTC = 4.55 (1200/269.60)

Price on January 1st 2016 - $433.57

Alan's Portfolio Value = 3.93*433.57 = $1704.02

John's Portfolio Value = 4.55*433.57 = $1974.37

Alan's ROI = 42%

John's ROI = 64.5%

So by using dollar cost averaging, John's average BTC purchase price was $269.60, whereas Alan bought a lump sum at $305.32. By having a lower average purchase price, John's ROI is higher over time. Alan bought her coins at the peak of the market before a prolonged downturn, whereas John utilized this downturn to his advantage.

Remember, time in the market beats timing the market. Generally speaking, the longer you are invested in something, the better.

FOMO & FUD

These are two terms you should become familiar with if you are going to be investing and trading in Bitcoin, or any cryptocurrency for that matter.

FOMO - Fear Of Missing Out

This is most commonly manifested when you see news reports of *<insert hot shiny new altcoin here>* increasing by ridiculous numbers like 100+% in a day. It may be tempting to trade a proportion or even all (terrible idea) your Bitcoin in for the latest cool cryptocurrency object, but it's incredibly risky. Many smaller altcoins are backed up by purely theoretical technology, and have no real world adoption for whatever product or service they are backing. Remember to do your due diligence regarding coin news. Just because the headline might read "Amazing Altcoin linked to Amazon deal", doesn't necessarily mean the deal is anywhere close, or if there even is a deal in the first place. Check your facts before investing.

It is important to understand that Bitcoin has now reached a point where there are real world uses, and it is by far the most adopted out of any cryptocurrency. Therefore, Bitcoin has greater market saturation and thus is unlikely to skyrocket in value like smaller coins. The opposite is also true though and with great rewards comes great risk. Many smaller coins can, and do lose up to 80% of their value in just a few days (for further reading check out the Chaincoin pump and dump scheme of July 2017), whereas Bitcoin continues to hold strong. If you are planning to buy and hold a single coin for the long term, Bitcoin should be your only play.

FUD - Fear, Uncertainty & Doubt

FUD is the spreading of misinformation by uninformed sources. Many of these sources have their own nefarious reasons for doing so. It may be to promote an alternative coin, or they may have shorted (bet on the price decreasing) Bitcoin. Of course, legitimate criticism of Bitcoin as a technology is fine, and should be encouraged if the technology is to advance. FUD however is mostly slander and baseless accusations about Bitcoin as a technology, the people behind it or the people invested in it.

How can you avoid FUD? Simply by obtaining your Bitcoin and other cryptocurrency news from reliable sources, who don't have a vested interest one way or another. It is important to use multiple sources to get a well rounded view of the situation.

Investing your Bitcoin - ICOs

An ICO or Initial Coin Offering, is an alternative form of crowdfunding that many blockchain startups have been utilizing as of late. Instead of donating in US Dollars in return for shares of the company, patrons can donate in Bitcoin or other cryptocurrencies in exchange for new tokens of the company.

The most famous ICO thus far was the Ethereum ICO of July 2014. Ethereum is a new blockchain based platform that allows applications and automatically executed contracts, known as "smart contracts" to be built on it. During the funding phase, Ethereum received roughly 31,500 Bitcoin, equivalent to $18.4 million at the time. In return, a total of 60 million Ethereum tokens were distributed to those who were part of the funding. The project has been extremely successful in the short term and today, 60 million Ethereum is worth approximately $24 billion.

ICOs represent a way for companies to fund their blockchain projects, in addition to providing returns for investors. Usually the offerings last for a period of a few weeks, and the company issuing the new tokens will have a goal amount that they aim to raise. ICOs have rapidly increased in popularity in the past 18 months, and 2017 is on track to be the first year that blockchain companies raise more money from ICOs than they do from traditional venture capitalists. For an investment purpose, ICOs represent a way for savvy investors to get in on the ground floor of an exciting new project.

The downside of this of course, is that with so many new ICOs popping up, some of them have far less legitimacy than others. If you are planning to invest in an ICO, do so based on the underlining usefulness of the project, and not any fancy marketing buzzwords that the company uses in their sales copy. Just because something is based on a blockchain platform, does not always mean there is a real world demand for the product or service. Another area to examine is the team of developers behind the project, and their track record of successfully developing blockchain applications.

Like any traditional startup venture, more ICOs will fail than succeed, and raising money is only part of a successful project. One such example of an ICO with problems is Bancor, an ICO based of the idea of creating a market-making (generating an automatic buy and sell price) product that provided liquidity for digital assets. The project raised a staggering $153m in just 3 hours, over 50% higher than the initial target.

However the project had problems with investor's transactions being accepted in addition to the Bancor team issuing extra token after the funding period was complete. This ultimately means a lower returns for investors. Like any investment, is important to do your due diligence before becoming involved, and never invest more than you can afford to lose. One final word, like anything in the Bitcoin or cryptocurrency space, ICOs are not a get rich quick scheme.

Lately the ICO buzz has been so intense that there are even ICOs utilizing Facebook Ads and celebrity endorsements in an attempt to gain investment. It's worth asking yourself if you would invest in a non-blockchain company based on a Facebook advertisement, and I think you already know the answer. If a company's main selling point is "amazing returns", rather than technological innovation, then it's likely to be a sub-par investment rather than a solid one.

The other area that is vital to understand, is that you ARE NOT buying stock in these companies during the ICO phase. You don't own any of the company, you simply own whatever token they denominize which will fluctuate in value due to external factors that go behind the company's own performance.

Why I Don't Recommend You Mine Bitcoin

Whenever Bitcoin's price is rising (and that's most of the time!), the mining question always pops up. Usually from those who are inexperienced or want a "free" way to get a piece of the pie.

It all starts with a variant of this question

"Why buy Bitcoin at $100/$1,000/$4,000 when you can just use your computer to mine some for free?"

Unfortunately, like everything else - there is no such thing as free Bitcoin.

As previously discussed, the way Bitcoins are created or "mined" is by using a computer to solve an of increasingly complex series of algorithms. Users are then rewarded for solving these algorithms by receiving Bitcoin. There is no man power involved, you yourself don't have to solve the algorithm, you just have to link your computer up to the Bitcoin network and the computer does the rest. There are also no shortcuts or breakthrough moments, the only way Bitcoin can be obtained quicker is with more computer power. How much computational power you supply determines the size of your reward. The more power you supply, the more Bitcoins you receive.

Now here is why mining is generally a terrible investment for the average Joe.

1. Electricity Costs - The electricity costs involved with running your computer 24/7 (which is necessary for mining) by far outweigh the amount of Bitcoins you receive for completing the task. You require access to industrial electricity rates of around $0.02 per kWh in order for the venture to be profitable on a small scale.

2. Requiring Specialist Hardware - Nowadays, the most efficient mining processes require special hardware known as Application-specific integrated circuits (ASIC). ASICs can be described as a supercomputer that can only ever perform one task. Specialist Bitcoin ASIC miners available for consumer purchase still start at around $1000 and often run around $2000-$2500.

3. Equipment maintenance - To maintain all this computing power is an additional cost. The cost of cooling alone is a large cost that has to be factored

in to long term profits. Hardware running 24/7 burns out faster and replacement mining equipment will be needed in due course.

4.   The increasing size of the Bitcoin network - The network pays out a fixed amount of Bitcoin, regardless of how many miners are using the network. The current rate is around 1800BTC per day, which sounds like a huge number, until you realise just how many miners there are on the network. The current mining power is equivalent to 17.6 BILLION desktop computers. Therefore the average payout for the end user running 1 desktop computer full time is around approximately $0.000107 per day. Or roughly 2 cents a year's worth of BTC. To put it lightly, you have more chance of winning the lottery than you do making a profit from mining Bitcoin your standard home computer.

Mining in 2017 is a much different proposition from mining in 2010 or even 2012. There are some opportunities which involved investing in Bitcoin farms or group purchasing processing power of ASIC at a discount. This is known as a "mining pool". Due to cheaper power costs, currently around 80% of the world's mining pools are based in China, with Iceland possessing the second largest number. Joining a mining pool requires a lower upfront investment but still requires cheap electricity rates and have debatable ROI potential.

It should also be worth noting that many of those who promote group mining or cloud mining do so under an affiliate program with whatever company that are promoting, meaning they get a commission % every time someone signs up.

However, for the average Joe without a huge amount of money to invest - I would strongly recommend buying coins instead of mining them. You are more likely to get higher returns in both the short and long run.

Is there a Bitcoin ETF or Mutual Fund I can invest in?

Exchange Traded Funds (ETFs) and mutual funds have represented some of the safest investments over the past few decades. Instead of investing in individual companies, you are buying an aggregate share of many companies. By allowing for this level of diversification, this represents a low risk use of your funds, and for many years investors have been clamoring for a Bitcoin or cryptocurrency fund like this due to the price volatility of individual cryptocurrencies.

Unfortunately attempts for a Bitcoin ETF have been thwarted by regulatory bodies thus far. In 2017, two Bitcoin ETF applications were rejected by the SEC. The reasoning from the government body was the lack of regulation and market surveillance in the cryptocurrency space.

The closest thing to a Bitcoin mutual fund today is a diversified fund offered by http://thetoken.io based out of Russia - the fund is a combination of 16 different cryptocurrency tokens, with Ethereum (22%) and Bitcoin (17%) representing the largest portions of the fund. Investments can be made with both BTC and ETH and funds are stored in Ethereum backed wallets. However, fiat currency investments are not currently supported. The fund is backed by a smart contract on the Ethereum platform to ensure the legitimacy of the tokens offered.

However, the main drawback of the site is that it is not available to those based in the US or Singapore, although this may change in the future based on the regulatory status of Bitcoin and other cryptocurrencies. Once again, like any investments you are liable to lose

money in a market downturn, so only invest money
you are comfortable losing.

The Ten Commandments of Bitcoin

If you get nothing else from this book, at least follow these rules and you'll be in a better position to make money than other new investors.

1. **Thou shalt believe in Bitcoin at a technological level**

2. **Thou shalt never gives one's private key to anyone else**

3. **Thou shalt always stay informed with Bitcoin news from reputable sources**

4. **Thou shalt never panic sell during a downturn**

5. Thou shalt always take intermediate profits for oneself

6. Thou shalt always store cryptocurrency safely

7. Thou shalt not spend every hour checking cryptocurrency markets

8. Thou shalt never mine Bitcoin on their regular desktop computer

9. Thou shalt not invest more than you can afford to lose

10. Thou shalt always help others with less knowledge than yourself

Conclusion

Bitcoin has changed the way we look at money and finance. Our previous reliance on banks and other financial institutions has been put into question. These long standing financial institutions now face unprecedented disruption from this groundbreaking technology. For users, cross border payments at a near-instant transaction time and far lower transactions fees are making the global economy smaller. For merchants, protecting themselves from fraud has never been easier with the rise of Bitcoin. Even non-profits can benefit hugely from Bitcoin as a payment method. Blockchain technology has an additional laundry list of benefits ranging from transparency in elections to easily accessible medical records between parties.

As a commodity, Bitcoin has produced unrivaled returns for investors over the past 7 years. No other financial asset, in the cryptocurrency space or otherwise has made more people money since its inception in 2010. For those who believe in Bitcoin, long may these returns continue.

I hope you've enjoyed this book and that you're now a little bit more informed about how Bitcoin works, and more importantly, how it can work for you. Whether you're planning on investing for the long-term, or hoping to make short-term gains by trading - I wish you the best of luck.

Remember, trade rationally and not emotionally. Never invest more than you can afford to lose, and for the love of God - don't check the charts 15 times a day.

If you're ready to make the next step and get involved in the market. I have a small gift for you.

Cryptocurrency: Insider Secrets - 12 Exclusive Coins Under $1 with Potential for Huge Profits in 2018

By Stephen Satoshi

Introduction - The state of the cryptocurrency market in November 2017.

Wow, what a year it's been. Bitcoin reaching all time highs of $7,400. Ethereum skyrocketing nearly 3000% in just 9 months and even Litecoin finally broke through it's seemingly unbreakable 2013 barrier to hit almost $95. These are exciting times in the cryptocurrency sphere. And the best is yet to come.

There is a HUGE amount of hype in the cryptocurrency market right now. If you look at the Google trends data you'll see giant rises in the popularity of cryptocurrency related searches. If you look at r/cryptocurrency, the official cryptocurrency subreddit, the number of subscribers increased from 25,000 at the beginning of the year to over 134,000 at the time of writing.

Unfortunately, with this increase in popularity, there has been an uptick in poor information and it seems like everyday there's another heavily hyped ICO or cryptocurrency project. We've started to see ICOs advertising on social media, and using celebrity influence to try and tap into the mind of the general public. These are the types of investments I have deliberately LEFT OUT of this book. I don't want anyone investing based on hype alone, or a cool Facebook ad featuring Floyd Mayweather or The Game.

In the research phase of this book I looked at over 50 different small market cap cryptocurrencies, read the white papers, checked out the development teams and investigated where they had real world usage potential. From this initial group I narrowed down the final selection to 12 coins. These are my personal "best of the rest" in the cryptocurrency market, and the ones with most growth potential in 2018.

The price of these coins is not the singular reason you should invest in them. The market capitalization figure is arguably more important. For example, Ripple (XRP) tokens are priced around $0.18 but has a market cap of around $6 billion, making it a far more mature and structured asset, with less potential for large gains in the future.

In terms of general investing advice, diversification is important. However, if you have been in the cryptocurrency market for any length of time, you will know just how quickly things can move. This is even more so the case with these small market cap coins. My personal recommendation (just my recommendation - this is not financial advice) is that you have no more than **30%** of your total cryptocurrency portfolio in small cap coins like this. The rest should be placed in more stable investments such as Bitcoin and Ethereum.

One final note, this book is written with the assumption that you have some basic knowledge of cryptocurrency and the ideas surrounding it. If you're a complete cryptocurrency novice, I recommend one of my other books *Cryptocurrency: Beginners Bible* as it explains even the most elementary of cryptocurrency concepts.

Thanks,

Stephen

Factors to Consider Before Investing

While larger cryptocurrencies like Bitcoin, Ethereum and Litecoin have long track records and multiple real world functions, some of the coins mentioned in this book do not - hence their lower price.

There are a number of different variables to investigate before you undertake any investment, and cryptocurrency has its own set.

Proof of Concept (PoC)

In other words, does the technology have a working model, or is it still in a theoretical stage. Obviously more mature coins will have a higher value, with the more theoretical coins being a bigger risk. As the different coins here are in different stages of their life cycle, that is up for you to decide.

The Development Team

Who are the developers and what is their track record.
Particularly within the cryptocurrency and blockchain
space? Another thing to consider their record within
the particular industry they are targeting.

The Utility Of The Coin

Ideas are great, but if the coin token itself doesn't have
usage, then the true potential of the project must be
questioned. This is especially true in the case of certain
coins where the theory and market potential checks
out, but the question of "why can I just use
Bitcoin/Litecoin to do the same thing" is often raised.

The Roadmap

Roadmaps are important for short-term gains because
they set out development targets for the coin. If these
goals are reached and the products/platforms move

from alpha to beta to a fully launched product, then that only means positive things for the coin and its value.

Which exchanges is the coin listed on

Many of these coins are still only available on smaller exchanges. Once the coin is listed on larger exchanges (for example Bittrex), the coin has greater visibility and this leads to a rise in value.

Mining Algorithm - Proof of Work vs. Proof of Stake

You'll notice later on when discussing individual coins that I talk about which mining algorithms are used. The two most popular are Proof of Work (PoW), used by Bitcoin and Proof of Stake (PoS), which will be used by Ethereum from Q4 2017 and beyond, and is currently used by a number of Ethereum based tokens.

In my previous book *Bitcoin: Beginners Bible* I discussed why I don't recommend mining as an effective method for obtaining cryptocurrency, for the regular user. That still holds true for the majority of the coins listed in this book, but it's important to understand why the difference in mining algorithm matters.

Why do we need mining?

We need mining to ensure a transaction (or block) is correctly validated, in order words, we need to ensure the same transaction doesn't occur twice - known as the double spending problem. As a reward for validating this transaction, miners are rewarded with a minute percentage of it (known as the network fee).

To put it bluntly, Proof of Work takes a lot more energy than Proof of Stake. A 2015 study showed that one

Bitcoin transaction takes the equivalent daily energy of 1.57 US homes. Proof of Stake is also a fairer, more energy efficient system, which is a huge advantage for community based coins.

Minimizing Your Risk with Dollar Cost Averaging

One of the best ways to minimize your risk in a volatile market is to use what is known as 'dollar cost averaging'. This simply means dividing up your total planned investment and buying cryptocurrencies at regular intervals instead of all at once.

With dollar cost averaging, you are simply buying less of an asset (for this example, I will use Bitcoin) when the price is high, and more when the price is low. Your total exposure is less because you are only exposed to part of any decline in the market, as opposed to all of it with a lump sum investment. Your average cost per coin is therefore likely to be lower.

Let's use an example, both Jamal and Rachel have $1200 to invest in Bitcoin at the start of 2015. Jamal decides to invest all $1200 on January 1st, Rachel on the other hand is going to use dollar cost averaging. She will invest $100 on the 1st of each month, for a total of $1200. The prices used in this example are the actual Bitcoin trading prices as of those dates.

January 1st 2015 - $305.32

February 1st 2015 - $237.18

March 1st 2015 - $263.57

April 1st 2015 - $255.23

May 1st 2015 - $226.45

June 1st 2015 - $233.44

July 1st 2015 - $260.73

August 1st 2015 -$283.04

September 1st 2015 - $229.00

October 1st 2015 - $240.10

November 1st 2015 - $325.28

December 1st 2015 - $375.95

Jamal's total investment in LTC = 3.93 (1200/305.32)

Rachel's total investment in LTC = 4.55 (1200/269.60)

Price on January 1st 2016 - $433.57

Jamal's Portfolio Value = 3.93*433.57 = $1704.02

Rachel's Portfolio Value = 4.55*433.57 = $1974.37

Jamal's ROI = 42%

Rachel's ROI = 64.5%

So by using dollar cost averaging, Rachel's average BTC purchase price was $269.60, whereas Jamal bought a lump sum at $305.32. By having a lower average purchase price, Rachel's ROI is higher over time. Jamal bought his coins at the peak of the market before a prolonged downturn, whereas Rachel utilized this downturn to her advantage.

Remember, time in the market beats timing the market. Generally speaking, the longer you are invested in something, the better.

Why you shouldn't touch a coin in the initial Post-ICO period

I made a conscious decision not to include any cryptocurrencies that were within 1 month of the end of their ICO. This particular period is extremely volatile price wise, and not a good period for anyone to enter the market, especially if you are an inexperienced cryptocurrency investor.

The reason for this volatility is often linked to ICOs offering a pre-sale bonus for early investors, who then sell their bonus in the post-ICO period for a quick profit, which ends up causing the price to fall. Usually, once the month after the ICO has ended, the price tends to become more stable.

All of the coins discussed in this book have been out of the ICO period for at least 1 month (many for years).

Investing during the ICO period is a different matter, if you choose to do so for future coins, I advise you to read any instructions carefully so you don't send any coins to the incorrect wallet address.

7 Giant Mistakes Guaranteed to Cost You Money

1. Not double checking all links (including the ones in this book)

Unfortunately, phishing scams are rife in the cryptocurrency space. Just this week, I saw 3 new ones either via email, paid search traffic (Google ads) or from reading about them on cryptocurrency message boards. Remember to check any link you click that is asking for you username, password or any other personal details.

2. Storing your cryptocurrency on an exchange

While rare, exchange attacks do happen, and cryptocurrency does get stolen. If you move your cryptocurrency off an exchange and into a private wallet, hackers cannot touch it (provided that wallet follows proper security measures). For each of the coins mentioned, I have included the appropriate wallet information for them.

3. Giving your private key to anyone

Your private key is what you need to send cryptocurrency from your wallet. You should never give this to anyone, for any reason. Keep it secure, preferably written on a piece of paper that is stored inside a physical safe. Never keep your private key on a server, and never enter it on a public Wi-Fi network.

4. Panic selling during a dip in the market

Unless you need the money to feed your family, there is ZERO reason to sell your cryptocurrency at a loss during a dip in the market. Remember, this investment should represent a small percentage of your overall investing portfolio, in other words - you can afford to take a small loss on paper. More often than not in the cryptocurrency market, waiting it out, and long term holding, is the best investment strategy.

5. Not using dollar cost averaging when buying

Time in the market beats timing the market. You can minimize your risk by using dollar cost averaging and spreading your investment out over time. This prevents getting burned by buying at the top of the market.

6. Not doing your research/due diligence

This book is designed to be a comprehensive introduction to these cryptocurrencies, but it is certainly not the only resource available. I encourage you to do your own research in addition to what I've provided in this book. The best source for information will come from the coin's own website and white paper (although at times white papers can read more like a press release than a technical document).

7. Borrowing money to invest in cryptocurrencies

This really should be obvious, but I've personally witnessed it too many times that I feel it needs to be reiterated. You should NEVER borrow money to invest in anything, let alone a market as volatile as cryptocurrency. Losing your own money is one thing, losing someone else's money is another. So, next time you're considering borrowing money from a bank, or using your student loan to invest - don't. Trust me, it's not worth it.

Bonus tip/mistake 7.5 - Checking the price of your investment on a daily basis

Just leave it alone - trust me

How to Buy Bitcoin

Gone are the days when buying Bitcoin was a time consuming and somewhat uncomfortable endeavor. Nowadays buying Bitcoin is a similar process to exchanging currency when you go on vacation.

There are two ways to buy Bitcoin, the first is to use fiat currency (USD, EUR, GBP etc.) to purchase cryptocurrency via an exchange. These exchanges function the same way as regular foreign currency exchanges do. The prices fluctuate on a daily basis, and like regular currency exchange markets - they are open 24/7. These exchanges make their money from charging a small fee for each transaction.

Some charge both buyers and sellers, some only charge a fee for buying. For security reasons, most of these exchanges will require you to verify your ID before allowing you to purchase cryptocurrency.

It is also important to note the type of payments each exchange supports. Some allow for debit/credit card payments whereas other only accept PayPal or bank wire transfers. Below are the three biggest and reputable currency exchanges for purchasing Bitcoin, Ethereum and other altcoins with fiat currency like US dollars, Euros or British Pounds.

Coinbase

Currently largest currency exchange in the world, Coinbase allows users to buy, sell and store cryptocurrency. Coinbase is undoubtedly the most beginner friendly exchange for anyone looking to get involved in the cryptocurrency market. They currently allow trading of Bitcoin, as well as, Ethereum and

LiteCoin using fiat currency as a base. Known for their stellar security procedures and insurance policies regarding stored currency. The exchange also has a fully functioning iPhone and Android app for buying and selling on the go, very useful if you are looking to trade.

Once you are signed up and complete the identity verification procedures you can buy Bitcoin with your credit or debit card instantly.

Coinbase also recently launched the Coinbase Vault, which is a secure way of storing your cryptocurrency while still having it accessible to trade. The vault uses double email address + phone verification in order to access your funds. If you're planning on holding long-term, I still recommend offline storage - but as an intermediary option, the Vault is a step in the right direction.

Note, if you're going to be trading Bitcoin, I recommend doing so on Coinbase's partner platform GDax, which has lower fees.

Bittrex

Based and regulated in the USA, Bittrex is a great exchange to buy altcoins for Bitcoin or Ethereum. With over 190 different cryptocurrencies, it is the most comprehensive in terms of altcoin support.

Their support isn't as good as Coinbase's, and you'll have to transfer the coins to a wallet if you want to securely store them long-term, but for trading altcoins - you can't go wrong with Bittrex.

Poloniex

With more than 100 different cryptocurrencies available and data analysis for advanced traders, Poloniex is the most comprehensive exchange on the market. Low trading fees are another plus, this is a great place to trade your Bitcoin into other cryptocurrencies. If you have never purchased Bitcoin before, you will no be able to do so as Poloniex does not allow fiat currency deposits. Therefore, you will have to make your initial Bitcoin purchases on Coinbase or Kraken.

Buying Locally

The second way to buy Bitcoins in exchange for fiat currency is to locally purchase them in person. The advantage of this is that you may be able to get a marginally better price than by using an exchange. The other advantage is that users living in countries that don't have easy access to online exchanges can still buy coins in person. All transactions are protected by Escrow to prevent either party being scammed.

Website http://localbitcoins.com is the current market leader for local bitcoin transactions with sellers in over 15,000 cities around the world.

Transferring your newly purchased Bitcoin to your exchange of choice.

Once you have bought your Bitcoin from Coinbase/Kraken, you'll need to then transfer it over the Binance, Bittrex or whichever exchange your coin of choice is listed on. To do this, simply go to the exchange you need to transfer the coins to (e.g. Bittrex) and click on "deposit", choose BTC (remember to double check you've clicked the correct coin). This will generate an address that looks like this

1F1tAaz5x1HUXrCNLbtMDqcw6o5GNn4xqX

From there, go to your Coinbase/Kraken BTC wallet and select "send", then in the "recipient" section copy the BTC address of the new exchange. Double check the amount of BTC you are sending, then click send and the transfer will initiate. Most of the time transfers take around 10 minutes, however some exchanges take longer to process. Once your transfer is complete you can then exchange your BTC for any of the altcoins listed below.

Storing Your Coins - How to set up MyEtherWallet

Many of these coins are based on the Ethereum blockchain, and therefore use ERC20 tokens. Therefore, these tokens can be stored in Ethereum wallets. Wallets can be daunting to set up at first, so I recommend you use something simple to get started, the most convenient of these is MyEtherWallet.

Step-by-Step guide to setting up MyEtherWallet

1. Go to https://www.myetherwallet.com/

2. Enter a strong but easy to remember password. Do not forget it.

3. This encrypts (protects) your private key. It does not generate your private key. This password alone will not be enough to access your coins.

4. Click the "Generate Wallet" button.

5. Download your Keystore/UTC file & save this file to a USB drive.

6. This is the encrypted version of your private key. You need your password to access it. It is safer than your unencrypted private key but you must have your password to access it in the future.

7. Read the warning. If you understand it, click the "I understand. Continue" button.

8. Print your paper wallet backup and/or carefully hand-write the private key on a piece of paper.

9. If you are writing it, I recommend you write it 2 or 3 times. This decreases the chance your messy handwriting will prevent you from accessing your wallet later.

10. Copy & paste your address into a text document somewhere.

11. Search your address on https://etherscan.io/ Bookmark this page as this is how you can view your balance at any time

12. Send a small amount of any coin from your previous wallet or exchange to your new wallet - just to ensure you have everything correct

Hardware Wallets

Another safe, offline solution is to use a hardware wallet. The most popular of these being Trezor and Nano S. Both of these cost around $100, but represent a convenient, yet safe way to store your cryptocurrency. Further explanation of hardware wallets is in my first book *Cryptocurrency: Beginners Bible*.

12 Exclusive Coins Under $1 with Potential for Huge Profits

District0x (DNT)

Price at Time of Writing - $0.039

Market Cap at Time of Writing - $23,255,100

Available on:

BTC: Binance, Bittrex, Liqui

Where to store:

District0x is currently an ERC20 token and can be stored on My Ether Wallet. You can view how to add DNT as a custom token on

https://etherscan.io/token/district0x

District0x has the goal of breaking the internet down into smaller, more manageable pieces. If you've ever seen the movie The Hunger Games, you'll remember each district was focused on a single task: District 7 was the lumber district, District 8 focused on textile production, District 9 with grain etc.

District0x plans to do the same thing with the blockchain technology and Decentralized Autonomous Organizations (DAO). Each district will have its own payment and invoicing system, along with complete self governance. The venture will use the Ethereum blockchain to run smart contracts.

What District0x has done to make to the process user friendly, is combine different necessary (like smart contracts and payment processing) elements into a package, so it's not essential for users to completely understand the technology behind the platform. At the core of every district is the ability to operate a market or a bulletin board application.

Currently, there are over 100 district ideas in play. Theoretically, it would allow an individual such as you or me to implement their own version of AirBNB, Craigslist or Uber, without having to go through a middleman like the current system has to. This in turn reduces transaction fees and makes the overall cost lower for all parties involved. There are no fees to create districts, which makes them available to everyone. Currently, refundable deposits are required to put forward a district proposal, once the district passes quality control checks (ensuring the district is not there for malicious intent), the deposit is refunded to the district creator.

One such idea already running is Ethlance, an online freelancing platform similar to Upwork or Fiverr, but without the large transaction fees. Interestingly enough, the DistrictOx team has actually hired developers via Ethlance to help them execute the project.

Another promising proposal is ShipIt, which focuses on the multi-billion dollar shipping industry. The idea is to create a decentralized maritime logistics platform. The sheer number of transactions in this industry alone (trucking, forwarding, warehousing etc.) make this is a perfect foil for a blockchain solution.

The framework is in place, however the team needs to do more to gather traction and a userbase to utilize their own districts. The current team is small, with just 10 members, plus an additional advisor, but there will certainly be additions in the future as the project continues to grow. Progress reports are frequent and developments are regular posted on GitHub.

One interesting approach the District0x team are employing is creating a free "education portal" to inform the wider public about the platform, and the real world functionality of districts. They are doing this are they believe the current limiting factor is a general ignorance of the potential of the platform. The portal is scheduled for rollout in Q4 2017.

District0x tokens (DNT) can be used to fund project and stake voting rights in different districts, the more tokens one has, the greater of a say they have. The one issue here is a possible abuse of a "pay to play" system.

The decentralized element of District0x means there is no single point of failure, for example there is no single server that all of the individual districts run from. This ensures that targeted hacking attacks cannot take down the entire network.

Supply wise, there are 600 million DNT available, with a total projected supply of 1 billion. It should be noted that in the white paper, the District0x team does reserve the right to add additional coins to the total supply, however this is contingent on the exchange rate between ETH/USD. For example, if ETH's value declines significantly vs. USD, the team can add additional coins to account for this fluctuation. This isn't necessarily something to be concerned about (financial hedging occurs all the time in fiat markets), but it's definitely something worth nothing.

Listing on larger exchanges will help spike the price in the short term. The team are in ongoing discussions with large exchange Bittrex, and a listing on there could easily see price rises of 100%. Long term prices will be largely determined by the number of popular districts that are set up using the platform. The next two planned district launches are Name Bazaar and Meme Factory.

Neblio (NEBL)

Price at Time of Writing - $0.984

Market Cap at Time of Writing - $12,220,794

Available on:

BTC: Cryptopia

Where to store?

Wallets can be downloaded from

https://nebl.io/wallets/

Based out of the USA, Neblio aims to provide a simple blockchain solution to the business sector. The project was born out of a need to simplify currently complex blockchain tools in order to achieve wider adoption within the business sector.

Taking into account blockchain solutions for transparent data, plus reliability and security owing to a lack of central server - the technology has a huge advantage for businesses over traditional methods. However, cost of maintenance, and difficulty of integration have made uptake in the business world somewhat slower than blockchain enthusiasts would like. Certain industries are waiting for more mature blockchain solutions to appear, rather than take a risk on technology that is unproven in their particularly sector. The Neblio team plan to streamline this process and make blockchain solutions more accessible for businesses as a whole.

A real world example of this would be a doctor's office needing to access patient records. Rather than use a traditional central database, that is liable to server downtime, or cyber attacks - they could use a blockchain solution which provides the same data, but without the risks. This same system could be used for any business that needs to utilize frequent audits, as the data would be unalterable with a record of who altered it and when.

Neblio plans to support current popular programming languages gives it a great advantage in this area. Developers in languages such as Python, Java, Javascript and PHP won't be forced to learn a new programming language to develop applications on the Neblio blockchain. This is an area that is vital if the platform wants to attract developers to Neblio versus other platforms. This also makes Neblio applications compatible with mobile devices running iOS or Android.

In terms of competitor coins, the space is extremely competitive. With giants such as Ethereum and Neo already occupying some of the real estate. Stratis is another big one, however, Stratis has had a year headstart and in terms of development, Neblio is already neck-and-neck.

The beta version of the Neblio network is currently scheduled for a launch in Q3 2018, with a larger scale marketing campaign due in Q2 of the same year. The team has been extremely active in developments, and recently both an iOS and Android wallet were both launched ahead of schedule.

Supply wise, there are approximately 12.5 million NEBL tokens in circulation currently, with a total supply of 13 million. NEBL tokens can be used as a means of exchange on the Neblio network

There is certainly a gap in the market for this type of blockchain solution. However, Neblio's future may lie with working within a specific industry, as the goal of solely providing broad "enterprise solution" is one that

is susceptible to a large amount of competition,
particularly from vast entities like Ethereum and Neo.

Bytom (BTM)

Price at Time of Writing - $0.069

Market Cap at Time of Writing - $80,324,168

Available on:

Fiat: Cryptopia (NZ)

BTC: Cryptopia, BTER (CN), Bit9 (CN)

Where to store?:

Bytom is currently an ERC20 token and can be stored on My Ether Wallet. You can view how to add Bytom as a custom token on Ethplorer via http://bit.ly/bytomwallet

Bytom is a true sleeper coin. Coming out of China, it's only natural that the coin has received initial comparisons to NEO (formerly Antshares), one of the most talked about cryptocurrencies of 2017.

Although their official Whitepaper is currently only available in Chinese, the roughly translated opening reads as "Bytom will not be another Bitcoin, or an Ethereum 2.0. Bytom is an intermediary connecting generalized blockchains with specialized blockchains." The whitepaper then goes on to discuss the idea of connecting physical and digital assets while resolving issues like compliance and trustworthiness.

In laymen's terms, Bytom has the potential for offline assets to be registered on the blockchain. In their own words, "bridging the online world and the atomic world". This bridging allows users to seamlessly swap between digital assets (like cryptocurrencies), and physical ones. This is something that no other cryptocurrency in development promises to utilize.

Real world applications for the technology include the management of income assets and dividend distribution for investors.

A very strong development team is headed up by Chiang Jia, who previously founded 8BTC - one of China's largest resources for cryptocurrency news and insights. Anyone who has been involved in the cryptocurrency market will understand just how important news from China is in affecting the price of Bitcoin and other crypto assets. The CEO was invited to speak at the 2017 Global Blockchain Summit.

Another determinant of the price is the viability of mining. Bytom has embraced the popular AI ASIC friendly mining algorithm. China is currently the world's largest base for cryptocurrency mining, with 70% of the entire mining work done in the Middle Kingdom. Part of Bytom's plan is to reward miners at a technological level as well as a financial one. CEO Jia stated in a June interview with 8BTC that "As for the mining industry, the outdated mining farm could be transformed into data center that provides AI hardware acceleration service." Chinese miners tend to support their own currencies, which is part of the reason for NEO's success in 2017. If Bytom can replicate this at even a fraction of the uptake, it will only mean good things going forward.

One particular thing to note about Bytom, is the team's dedication to continued, if somewhat slow progress. However, you can look at this in a positive light. Rather than succumbing to spending their entire budget on marketing like other coins, Bytom's roadmap is well laid out with realistic goals. You don't need to expect life changing developments within the next 6 months for example. But a solid alpha product in Q1 2018 could certainly lead to decent short term gains. Right now, the scheduled release of v1.0 of the Bytom blockchain is due in Q2 2018.

Other notable figures include Long Yu, a former Senior System Engineer at Alipay, a huge Chinese POS payment system (similar to Apple Pay or Samsung Pay).

In early September the Bytom team took home 2nd prize in a field of over 100 competitors in the 2017 Cosmos Hackathon, a blockchain network designed to solve problems like scalability and interoperability. 2nd Place is currently the best achievement from a Chinese team at the competition.

The roadmap shows that by early 2018, many of Bytom's most exciting features will be put to market, in beta form. A large press conference for the release of their alpha product is scheduled for Q1 2018.

Currently Bytom is in a unique place where there are no strict competitor coins.

The have been some blips in the development stages already, with Bytom removing the coin from Binance in mid August. However the coin is now listed on Cryptopia, which while being a small exchange compared to giants like Bittrex and Poloniex, does make it accessible to the US and western market. The Chinese market has easy access with direct BTN/CNY trades available on the BTC9 exchange. Those holding ETH can exchange it for Bytom at the BTER exchange.

Bytom's value comes from the fee each user will have to pay to use the Bytom blockchain. Holding Bytom coins essentially represents shares in the blockchain itself. Bytom believes strongly in this community based ownership model, and their concept of "distributed autonomy" is one that they hold dearly to the project. The aim is structure the management system for a balance between efficiency and fairness.

Circulating supply is high at 664 million BTN currently available, with a projected total supply of 2.1 billion BTN. Of this total supply, 7% is reserved for private equity groups and angel investors, whose funds will be used in the technology's initial development stages.

Overall, Bytom might not make any major price movements in the next 3 months, but as soon as 2018 rolls around, the coin has potential to make a big impact in the blockchain space.

Note: On some cryptocurrency exchanges, Bitmark will be listed as BTM, these two currencies as not related. Double check before executing a trade.

Golem (GNT)

Price at time of writing - $0.267

Market Cap at time of writing - $222,516,176

Available on:

Fiat: Yunbi (CN)

BTC: Poloniex, Bittrex, Liqui

Where to store?

Golem is an ERC20 token so can be stored in MyEtherWallet

Golen is a coin token, based on Ethereum blockchain technology. With nearly 10 months since the original ICO, Golem is somewhat of a granddad in the cryptocurrency world. Described by some commentators as the "AirBNB of computing", the value of the coin is centered around the tasks that can be accomplished using it.

The founders of the Golem Project refer to it as a "supercomputer", with the ability to interconnect with other computers for various purposes. These include scientific research, data analysis and cryptocurrency mining. For example, if your computer has unused, or idle power, using the Golem network, you can rent that power (hence the AirBNB comparison) to someone else who needs it. The user who needs the extra power, has the ability to access supercomputer levels of processing power for a fraction of the cost of actually owning the processing power themselves. Like other Ethereum based projects, the decentralized element provides an additional layer of security as there is no single point of failure on the network. The first use case of the network's alpha release was using shared processing power to produce a 3D CGI rendering.

One fantastic potential usage for this power is the ability for a company to prevent downtime during a urge of users. There are many examples of websites being down during periods of unusually high demand, such as waiting for a livestream of a popular event to start. One notable example of this is Rockstar's website crashing during the release of the Grand Theft Auto 4 trailer. Using idle power from other computers on the Golem network, has the potential to prevent issues like this from occurring in the future.

The growth of such services is currently in demand in the non-crypto space, with cloud computing services accounting for roughly $175 billion global turnover in 2015. For example, Amazon's Amazon Web Services (AWS) business is an increasing part of the online giant's overall holdings.

If you look at Golem vs. Traditional cryptocurrency mining, Golem is definitely a step ahead. Because it only utilizes idle power, there is no wasted energy, which traditional mining suffers from a lot of. Even for a casual user, the ability to offset some of their electricity costs is a big positive.

The ability for users to earn money for their unused computing power is, in theory, a no-brainer, however what remains to be seen is the practical application of the technology. The Golem team's lack of marketing visibility also appears to hurt the coins value in recent times. The lack of ability to buy GNT using fiat currency (such as USD) is also a drawback for the mass market, however for small cap coins, that is somewhat of a given at this stage of the overall cryptocurrency lifecycle.

Supply wise, 1 billion GNT tokens were generated during the ICO, and that is the sum total that will be available for the lifetime of the project. Tokens will be used as a transfer of value on the Golem network.

It should be noted that the technology is still very much in the early development stages and as of August 2017, the team are still looking for alpha testers for the project. The Golem Project has a very real possibility of petering out into nothing. On the flip side - there is tremendous potential for large future gains with the price of a coin still under $0.30.

Tron (TRX)

Price at time of writing - $0.0018

Market Cap at time of writing - $125,420,800

Available on:

BTC: Liqui

ETH: Liqui, EtherDelta

Even in small and medium cap cryptocurrencies, Tron is a true wildcard. Lead by Justin Sun, known in China as "The next Jack Ma", and part of Forbes Asia 30 Under 30 - the project is one with wide reaching implications for the in-app currency movement.

You can think of Tron as both a facilitator for in-game or in-app transactions (also known as microtransactions) and as a way of increasing the value of your own content.

The biggest trend in video games for the past 5 years has been the rise in in-game microtransactions, also known as the pay-to-win model. This frustrates gamers as any assets they have built up in game 1, are not transferrable to game 2. For example, take the popular mobile game Clash of Clans. The game features a huge amount of microtransactions, and players have spent hundreds of dollars building up their in-game assets. Currently there are only very limited ways for him to sell those assets in exchange for money. Plus, if a new game comes out and the gamer wants to try it out, they'd have to start from the bottom and work their way up again. Tron would allow said gamer to transfer his Clash of Clans assets over to the new game in exchange for a small transaction fee.

Content creators can also use Tron as a payment system for their content. Similar to how YouTube users use Patreon donations as a method of making additional income from their content.

The development team continues to grow, and the recent announcement of one of Alibaba's (the Amazon of China) chief engineers joining the project is another coup for the Tron team.

The future of Tron will depends of two things. The first is adoption, which games will support TRX as a middleman for cross-game transactions? Secondly would these games choose TRX over the coins currently available like BTC or LTC. Like many of the coins mentioned in the book, they idea in theory is a multi-billion dollar one, but does the token have enough utility to warrant it?

Supply wise, Tron is huge. With over 40 billion TRX coins currently in circulation, with a projected total of 100 billion. However, as the coin is designed to facilitate microtransactions (fractions of a cent), a large supply is needed.

In a show of good faith, in early October 2017, the Tron team air dropped 500 TRX coins into the wallet of everyone with an account on the exchange liqui.io. Air drops like this have useful community building and general awareness effects.

Aeon (AEON)

Price at time of writing - $0.84

Market Cap at time of writing - $12,359,745

Available on:

BTC: Bittrex

If you've read my first book *Cryptocurrency: Beginners Bible*, you'll remember I talked about Monero (the price has risen 3x since the release) being the only truly private cryptocurrency currently on the planet. Well, that's no longer the case. You can think of Aeon as Monero's little brother. In a market of overhyped, overbought ICOs and heavily marketed copycat projects, AEON brings lightweight innovation - the coin is a mobile-friendly, decentralized digital currency.

The team behind Aeon feature some of the core Monero developers - in the words of Aeon's founders "everybody's main internet device continues to be their cellphone, a device with a low-powered CPU and limited available storage. AEON is about enabling this era, enabling an age where all people everywhere have the freedom to privately send and receive money with whatever gadget they already own."

By focusing on smaller transactions like this, Aeon aims to take a firm hold on the daily consumer market, all while offering a completely private service. So why the need for privacy? Frankly, many of us are sick and tired of our data being stored on central servers, privy to anyone that wants to take a look. Aeon uses cryptography to completely encrypt the information of both the sender and receiver in a transaction. Therefore, the identifying information of each user is not available on the blockchain itself. This is compounded with what is known as "ring signatures", which means the funds are untraceable.

Aeon will often be compared to Monero, however the faster blockchain verifications (thanks to their lighter weight Proof of Work algorithm) allow transaction to process faster, making it more useful for day-to-day use. You could look at the relationship similar to Litecoin's relationship with Bitcoin.

The lightweight features of Aeon allow users to run a full node on their mobile, this speeds up transactions due to no longer needing a third party app running a public node. Another addition area where Aeon shines is by using a limited amount of storage space on a given device, this reduces the likelihood of any age-based attacks on your mobile or laptop.

One area that could be seen as a drawback for Aeon is the lack of a publicly released roadmap. This is due to an extremely small development team, of officially just 1 person at the time of writing. However, Aeon's open source code is publicly available, and everyone is welcome to contribute to the project, in a similar vein to Monero - which benefited greatly from a enthusiastic community. A community generated development fund currently stands at over $400,000 - which is far higher than other coins with much larger market caps. This fund will be used to attract elite developers to the project in the short and medium term.

Supply wise, Aeon has a relatively small number of coins released at around 14.5 million. For those into mining, Aeon currently offers some of the better rewards in the cryptocurrency mining space, plus in theory their lightweight nodes could allow for efficient mobile mining (albeit for significantly reduced rewards).

Where Aeon's future growth may lie is a release their mobile wallet in the short term and wider adoption of private cryptocurrencies in the long term. This is one coin that certainly has gamechanging potential.

RISE (RISE)

Price at Time of Writing - $0.401

Market Cap at Time of Writing - $45,404,571

Available on:

Fiat: Litebit.eu (EUR)

BTC: Bittrex, YoBit

Where to store?

You can download RISE wallets for desktop (Windows, Mac and Linux) from the Rise website http://rise.vision

RISE is an ecosystem for developers, businesses, tech startups, investors and device users. The platform offers decentralized applications and the creation of smart contracts. The platform aims to increase adoption of RISE versus competitor platforms by providing Software Development Kits (SDKs), so that RISE applications can be run on Windows, Mac and Linux. The platform also supports popular programming languages like Javascript, Python and Ruby. There's also a RISE investment platform where RISE holders can pool resources together to invest in projects.

Where RISE really shines is their "blockchain incubator" service for startup Decentralized Apps (DApps). These developers can use the RISE platform to develop their companies/coins, and RISE holders will be entitled to 20% of these coins when the product successfully launches. While RISE isn't the first cryptocurrency to offer a form of passive income like this, a 20% reward is far higher than competing coins.

The two current projects built using the RISE platform are Interlet and Chipz. Interlet is an Ethereum based person-to-person vacation platform that aims to compete with AirBNB, by charging a much lower fee to operate. Anyone who has used AirBNB in the past will know about often ridiculous fees (up to 20% of the vacation price) that AirBNB takes as a middleman, and Interlet plans to use this is a basis for providing competition.

The second project is Chipz, an online casino platform due for launch in Q1 2018. Those who hold RISE will be given a % of Chipz tokens based on how much RISE they hold at the time of launch. Chipz plans to integrate with the Waves platform so that holders of the token can directly exchange their Chipz for fiat currency, which in theory will make the casino a lot more accessible. A successful launch of Chipz will certainly mean good things for the price of RISE in the short term.

Competition wise, RISE can be compared to Ark and Lisk in broad terms. However, RISE offers token holders a much bigger share of DApp coins launched on the platform at 20% when compared to Ark's 5%.

The roadmap is an area where RISE is lacking when compared to other coins mentioned in this book. Projects are in the pipeline, including the release of Interlet, as well as a mobile friendly version of RISE. However, a lack of dates for these releases is something that the RISE team needs to address to inspire investor confidence.

That being said, the RISE team is a strong one, with 10 developers, many of which have a long and successful history in the blockchain and cryptocurrency space. One area I particularly like is the weekly release of a RISE newsletter, these 4 page posts give updates on the RISE ecosystem, as well as announcing team members, and any new projects in development. Easily digestible new bites like this are useful if you don't come from a tech or development background, or are more interested in the business side of things.

The RISE community continues to grow rapidly, and often times community driven initiatives can help maintain and increase the coin's value over time.

Supply wise, RISE currently has 114 million tokens in circulation. The utility of these tokens has already been discussed, and there are strong use cases both as voting tools and as a currency to be traded. The trading volume is very high for a coin of RISE's size, and this bodes well for it as an investment tool as it is less susceptible to price manipulation than coins with lower trading volumes.

Funfair (FUN)

Price at Time of Writing - $0.026

Market Cap at Time of Writing - $100,375,472

Where to store?

FUN tokens are ERC 20 tokens, so you can add them to MyEtherWallet by using the following information:

Address:

0xbbb1bd2d741f05e144e6c4517676a15554fd4b8d

Token symbol: FUN

Decimal places: 8

Funfair is a decentralized gaming platform powered by Ethereum smart contracts, based out of London and Singapore. Powering the creation of "smart casino", the platform is attempting to capitalize on the potential $40 billion a year online gambling industry, an industry which has increased by 50% since 2010 and in projected to increase by another 50% by 2020.

The platform's main aims are to facilitate the building of online casinos with 3D games that can be built with current technology (namely HTML5) for both desktop and mobile platforms. In terms of gas costs (Ethereum transactions fees), these will be up to 10x cheaper than current online casino platforms.

As the games are executed with the use of Ethereum smart contracts, their fairness is not in question. The random number generated is transparent on the blockchain so anyone can see the results are truly randomized, and not artificially in favor of the house. This ensures that no one is being cheated by the casino operator.

Cryptocurrency gaming in itself is not a new phenomenon, in fact Bitcoin casinos have been running for years. However, the fluctuations in the currency itself, along with notoriously slow payouts and lack of regulation, has yet to see mainstream adoption.

The development team is built largely of members with previous experience in game creation. Founder and Angel Investor Jez San has a storied history in the gaming sector and helped play a part in the creation of multi-million dollar selling video games like Star Fox, while recently his experience lies in the online gaming space at leading online poker website PKR.com, before leaving the site to focus on Funfair. These connections could play a vital role in the adoption of Funfair within the gaming space, which is undoubtedly the number one challenge it faces going forward.

There are already complete 3D games built using the platform, which means the technology is now firmly beyond the theoretical stage, and into the execution stage. The Funfair launch suite itself already has 6 games under construction, which will be used as playable prototypes at industry events.

It is important to note that Funfair's value will not just come from the operation of 1 casino. Licensing the software itself will potentially create thousands of online casinos, which in turn will be in significantly more revenue than a centralized model. However, the challenge of getting that initial casino to decide to use the platform is a large one.

The main problem that has previously plagued this sector the transaction fees that occur with every new game or spin. This has led to other blockchain casinos suffering from slow playing times and costly fees to play. After all, nobody wants to have to wait 30 seconds between blackjack hands or between dice rolls for roulette. There's also a limit with the number of players that can play at one time. Current technology has a general rule of about 10 players per table, whereas with blockchain technology, the number, in theory, is unlimited.

The transactions costs are estimated to be at a ridiculous $1 per hand for blockchain based blackjack games and $0.75 per bet on dice games. With typical bet sizes, this represents around 10% per hand. Transactions costs have a further effect, because of the house edge of casino games. Even with higher bets minimizing the cost per hand, the house edge + transaction costs are simply too large for the player to even have a chance of profiting in the long term. Funfair's aim to reduce these will lead to a much higher uptake from players. One of Funfair's key goals is to reduce player transaction costs to a much more manageable 0.1% per hand.

Supply wise, over 3 billion FUN tokens were generated in the ICO - with no further token due to be generated during Funfair's life cycle . The sounds like a large number, however it is important to note that many of this are designed to be "burned" as transaction fees for the games themselves.The FUN token value itself will be utilized in a number of ways. Including for playing the games themselves, paying affiliates (which is a significant part of the online casino industry), and paying the game creators themselves.

Mothership (MSP)

Price at Time of Writing - $0.167

Market Cap at Time of Writing - $23,389,520

Where to store?

MSP token are ERC20 tokens so can be stored on

MyEtherWallet

Mothership is one of the most intriguing

cryptocurrencies on the market today. Built on the

Ethereum platform, the coin's aim is to make

cryptocurrency markets accessible for EU companies

and Estonian e-Residents.

To truly understand Mothership, it's important to first

understand Estonian e-residency, and how that

process works.

E-residency takes place in the form of an Estonian government issued "digital ID card", which is combined with an authorized digital signature. The signature is legally binding and allows anyone in the world to register an EU company online. This gives unprecedented access to the European market. In a time where previously repressed parts of the world are looking for ways to attract new business and investment, Estonia is certainly at the forefront of this movement.

Where Mothership comes in, is that for blockchain businesses, it allows incorporation in Estonia, with 100% remote online access. A bank account will be provided, which is then linked with the built-in cryptocurrency exchange. Estonia also offers 0% corporation tax for companies inside the e-residency scheme. This is an extremely attractive proposition for blockchain companies that were previously forced to operate in countries with less friendly regulation, both in terms of the legality of cryptocurrency based firms, and general business tax laws.

The project entails three parts. A cryptocurrency exchange with 24/7 access to the markets, which combined with automatic identification (linked to your e-residency) makes the transactions from cryptocurrency to fiat currency near instant. Anyone who has signed up to a cryptocurrency exchange will know the pains of having to wait days (or even sometimes months) for identity verification.

The built-in cryptocurrency wallet is connected to your e-residency, which provides an automatic digital signature, which in turn protects your funds from fraudulent activity.

The e-residency program continues to grow, and Estonia estimates more than 10 million e-residents by

2025. Government support is one area that many crypto-based assets lack, whereas Mothership has been truly embraced by the Estonian government.

The project's timeline is publically available to view on Trello. The short-term goals include launching the beta version of the MSP token market whereas the actual exchange itself is planned for a launch between Q1 and Q2 2018. This is also the time period where the team plans to launch the e-residence wallet.

Supply wise, there will are currently 140 million MSP tokens, with an additional 60 million planned in the future.

The inherent risk to the Mothership project is that they are not specifically offering anything *new* to the market. There are already hundreds of cryptocurrency exchanges. However, the tie-in with the e-residency scheme, and the instantaneous swapping between cryptocurrency and fiat makes the project an attractive one in the short-to-medium term at the very least.

OKCash (OK)

Price at Time of Writing - $0.317

Market Cap at Time of Writing - $23,143,613

Where to store?

You can download the official OKCash wallet (available for both desktop and Android) from https://okcash.org/

Available on:

Fiat: Litebit.eu (EUR)

BTC: Bittrex, Cryptopia

Dubbing itself "the future of cash", OKCash plans to operate a worldwide payment system for microtransactions. With no cross-border payments and near instant confirmation times, the platform plans to target those in countries where bank account usage is not widespread. In other words, people have the ability to make payments to one another without needing a bank account.

The low-fee system allows OKCash to be useful for small donations or even online tipping. These tips can be made public and donations can be made over social networks for greater visibility. This could even be used in the case of emergencies to transfer funds fast to those affected.

While other cryptocurrencies promise similar things with regard to microtransactions and quick payments, where OKCash shines is the extremely low payment fee. There is no fee to receive a payment and the current fee to send OK coins is just 0.0001 OK, or $0.00003

One cool feature of the OKCash wallet is a built-in encrypted messaging system to protect users privacy.

OKCash has seen some strong initial adoption, with over 136,000 OKCash wallets being created already, and more than 19,000 addresses holding at least 1000 OK coins.

The proof-of-stake mining algorithm ensures minimal wasted energy when compared to a traditional proof-of-work algorithm (used by Bitcoin). The decentralized model also allows anyone to contribute to the OKCash network.

The team's marketing efforts have been unique and quite successful so far. A focus on video games has led to OKCash being a prize in both Minecraft and FIFA tournaments so far, with more projects like this to come in the near future.

The development team, and their lack of public visibility is an area that OK is lacking in. Although their site lists more than 40 team members, all of them currently go by pseudonyms, which is not helpful if the coin wants to achieve wider adoption.

Supply wise, there are roughly 72 million OK in existence currently. This number is deliberately larger than some other currencies in order to facilitate micro payments.

Note: OKCash is not to be confused with the Chinese Bitcoin exchange OKCoin.cn - double check any news regarding OKCash

Status (SNT)

Price at Time of Writing - $0.022

Market Cap at Time of Writing - $76,414,847

Available on:

Fiat: BTC9 (CN), b8wang (CN)

BTC: Bittrex, Liqui

Where to store?

Status users ERC20 tokens so can be stored using MyEtherWallet.

Status is an intriguing project that focuses on the mobile space. Based out of Switzerland, it's a free, open source mobile client targeting Android and iOS. The platform itself is built on Ethereum technology. Currently the platform supported 30 languages including Chinese, Korean and Russian. The main focus of the Status project in terms of high level goals is providing a fully private platform, with focus on a lack of censorship and economic transparency.

Co-Founder Jarrad Hope stated "One way to think about Status is that it'll eventually serve as a sort of onramp or gateway so that everyday people can benefit from decentralized applications built on Ethereum, whilst simultaneously helping DApp developers to reach new users."

Status users can search and discover decentralized apps (DApps). Similar to how one would do so on the Apple Store or the Google Play Store on their smartphone now. Examples of these apps include the freelancing platform Ethlance and Ujo, which is a decentralized music licensing and distribution platform. Status definitely have first mover advantage when it comes to a platform like this.

The other main usage here would be a decentralized peer to peer trading market. Similar to how localbitcoins.com currently operates. If Status can provide this for Ethereum based tokens, it could potentially be a game changer for the platform as a whole.

The aim of all this is to provide a digital hub where users only need one identity, as opposed to various usernames, passwords and apps that are common in the current system.

Status also featurs a built-in messenger with encrypted messaging and the ability to send Ethereum payments between parties, as well as smart contracts. The team chose to focus on messaging first and foremost, as they believed that this was the best and most efficient way to achieve mass market potential. Instant messaging software also has the highest install, and lowest uninstall rate of any mobile software.

The community element is a strong core belief of the platform. Status tokens (SNT) can also be used to ask questions to prominent community members, similar to how one would ask questions on the website Quora. Users can set a minimum number of SNT required to send them a message. This could lead to the rise in "celebrity users" with high levels of SNT required to contact them.

The team also offers rewards for those who can uncover bugs in their code. So far, the team has developed a fully functioning alpha product, with the help of over 6,000 testers.

In terms of competitors,you can think of Whatsapp as being the application with broad similarities to Status.

The growth and true potential of Status will depend on the adoption of DApps as a whole, because it's unlikely that it's true calling will be purely as a mass-adopted chat app like Whatsapp or WeChat. If the team can facilitate a DApp store, then there is indeed a lot of room for growth in the coming years. In terms of cryptocurrency based competitors, kik is the one that is likely to be competition to Status in the short term.

One thing to factor with Status, is that first time movers often do not have a long-term advantage. The growth of Status will depend solely on their ability to stay ahead of the market, which is tough when competitors could come in and exploit Status' weaknesses as a platform.

Unlike other cryptocurrency projects, Status was self-funded for the first two years of its life. Supply wise, Status has a total supply of 6 billion, with 41% of this being funds contributed by the public during their

July ICO. Interestingly enough, their ICO was designed so that large investments could not dominate the holdings. The Status team actually refunded more ETH than they took in during the ICO period.

The team are very active on their Slack channel (which currently has over 15,000 members), which is something that can't be said for some of the other coins mentioned in this book. Like any complex project, transparency is always a good thing, especially in times when there may not be much to report on the development front.

In terms of roadmap, Status is aiming for a public release towards the end of 2018, or beginning of 2019 - making this a good opportunity to get involved before then. A beta release in the middle of 2018 would give a clearly indication of the long term potential of Status, both as a platform, and as a messaging system.

Tierion (TNT)

Price at Time of Writing - $0.081

Market Cap at Time of Writing - $34,638,811

Available on:

BTC: Liqui, HitBTC (CN),

ETH: EtherDelta

Tierion aims to use blockchain technology as a data verification platform. Using their open source timestamping proof Chainpoint - Tierion has the ability to verify the integrity of a file, record, or process - without having to rely on a third party.

The practical applications for this are widespread. The ability to issue digital receipts for purchases, insurance claims or stock trades, which act as an immutable proof of purchase is a great asset in fighting fraudulent chargebacks and fraudulent transaction claims.

For auditors, the ability to timestamp data with a proof of record will drastically lower the chances for people to go back into a database an alter it. For example, a situation like Enron would not be allowed to happen with data stored on the blockchain. Going one step further, the auditing industry as a whole faces a huge threat from blockchain solution such as Tierion

Medical records, legal records are other areas where blockchain's verification process could have great benefits for society at large in the future.

Many of the above examples are ones that don't just apply to Tierion, but blockchain technology as a whole. That being said - why Tierion?

The answer is simple, speed. Tierion's API lets developers add up to 100 records per second, this is far quicker than previous blockchain solutions. An additional big advantage is their usage of current technology to make the process user friendly. It is much easier to create data stores using HTML forms which are both desktop and mobile compatible, than it is to learn an entire new programming language just for this purpose. This bridge between generations of technology, has great usage potential in the blockchain space for the near future.

Another cool thing about Tierion is its integration with widely used applications such as Salesforce, Gmail, Google Docs, and Mailchimp.

Unlike many of the blockchain based firms in this book, Tierion also has a full functioning product, which you can actually sign up to use for free today. The free version is limited to 15,000 data records per month, which should be more than enough for the average home user. Obviously, from a business standpoint, the money will be made with the Enterprise versions of the software.

The project already has links with some larger multinational companies. An invitation to join Dutch electrical giant Phillips' Blockchain Lab, a thinktank dedicated to see how blockchain technology can be used in healthcare. January 2017 bought an announcement of a working agreement with Microsoft to use blockchain technology to prove data existence and validity.

The big question with Tierion, is the utility of the TNT token itself. Will TNT be adopted as part of the Tierion ecosystem, or will users still prefer to carry that their transactions using a different cryptocurrency.

First Blood (1ST)

Price at Time of Writing - $0.517

Market Cap at Time of Writing - $44,310,766

Available on:

BTC: Bittrex, Liqui

Built on the Ethereum platform and based out of Boston with heavy ties to China, First Blood focuses on the ever growing esports space. First Blood aims to build a blockchain support esports platform that will allow gamers from around the world to compete against one another for prizes.

The use of smart contracts will ensure all results are fair and just, and that no cheating can occur. For those not in the know, the esports world has been plagued by cheating scandals ever since cash prizes were first introduced.

Their marketing efforts have been solid to say the least, and their "from the ground up" marketing strategy includes offering sponsorships to video game live streamers.

In terms of game themselves, First Blood's main focus for now is on the extremely popular Multiplayer Online Battle Arena game DOTA2 - with other game support planned for the future

An already established relationship with blockchain video game developer MOLD was compounded by a huge announcement on October 2nd 2017.

"We are proud to announce we will be working with the Chinese Government and Chinese esports companies to organize esports tournaments!"

More specifically, they're going to be used by the General Administration of Sport of China., the government agency responsible for sports in China. In a statement on their website the team announced

"First Blood will be a partner for hosting the Chinese University Esports League (CUEL). CUEL is a huge competition in China and each year hundreds of thousands of students participate.The partnership with First Blood was put into place as CUEL aimed to reduce their overheard."

The full version of the platform isn't out yet, but previous developer updates have mentioned banning cheaters from the beta platform, which shows that the technology is working at a basic level at least.

Future plans for the coin include support for additional popular games such as League of Legends and Counter Strike: Global Offensive - making this coin one to watch as we move into 2018

2Give (2GIVE)

Price at Time of Writing - $0.0053

Market Cap at Time of Writing - $2,786,042

Available on:

BTC: YoBit, Bittrex

Where to store?

The 2Give team currently has desktop wallets for Windows and Mac available on their website. A Linux wallet is coming soon.

2Give (or GiveCoin 2.0) is a comparatively tiny project when compared to some of the larger ones discussed here like Bytom and Status. With a market cap of just under $3 million dollars, it's safe to say that this one is a long shot indeed, but it's one with a good cause at heart, which is why it made the cut for this book.

From the official website "2GIVE makes it easy to support your favorite non-profit or pro-social cause and can be used for "repaying it forward" through social tipping!" The coin is supported by the Strength in Numbers Foundation, a non-profit digital trust. The idea is that user can donate to their charity of choice, without giving a significant portion of the funds to a payment process, while simultaneously revealing their online identity.

As previously mentioned, 2Give is the newer version of what was known as GiveCoin. The reason for the switch is that GiveCoin suffered from "pool hoppers", miners who switched between mining chains because it was financially advantageous to do so. This led to a system where the top 2% of GiveCoin miners took home most of the mining profits. 2Give's switch to a

Proof of Stake model allows fairness to be restored among the mining community.

2Give attracts miners with a social conscience with their reward system, which offers a 5% to miners and stakeholders who help keep the platform operational. Miners then get an additional 1% as a transaction fee for processing payments on the 2Give network.

Many online rumours are flying around regarding 2Give's partnership with a number of large companies, including online streaming service Twitch and even UNICEF. It should be noted that with a market cap as small as this, these rumours can and do have a significant effect on the price.

2Give has received some early adoption, including a partnership with the Japanese Bitcoin ATM network coinoutlet. Coinoutlet ATM users can now buy 2Give at any of the ATM's around the country.

Future plans for the coin include mobile wallets for both iOS and Android, as well as a real world "air drop" in which gift cards will be left in various location to spread awareness of 2Give. The growth of 2Give will be determined largely by the adoption of the idea from non-profits around the world. If larger ones do get involved, then 2Give tokens will therefore have more utility and increase in price accordingly.

Conclusion

Well there we have it. 12 altcoins under $1 that have HUGE potential for gains in the next 12-18 months.

I hope this information has been beneficial to you and has given you a foundation to invest some of the more unknown cryptocurrencies. There has never been a more exciting time for cryptocurrencies than right now, so there's no better time to get involved.

I encourage you to do additional research before investing in any of these, particularly by checking out the white papers on the individual coin websites, which will give you a much more in-depth look at the technology behind them.

Remember to invest wisely (with your own money), don't check your investments on a daily basis, and don't panic sell if you see a dip in the market.

I wish you the best of luck in the cryptocurrency market, and I hope you make a lot of money.

Finally, if this book has proved useful to you, I'd appreciate it if you took 2 minutes to leave it a review on Amazon.

Thanks,

Stephen

Blockchain Beginners Bible:

Discover How Blockchain Could Enrich Your Life, Your Business & Your Cryptocurrency Wallet

By Stephen Satoshi

Introduction

Hi, I'm Stephen and I'm a blockchain addict.

Well, enthusiast is probably a better term - although I still definitely check my cryptocurrency portfolio far too frequently.

I've certainly come a long way from the young man who first heard about this Bitcoin thing back in the 2010s. You know, that new internet currency that people were making money from.

How could a currency be worth anything if it isn't backed by a central government? Oh, how naive I was.

This initial exposure to Bitcoin sparked an interest in blockchain technology and it's potential. I try to refrain from hyperbole but I truly believe this is mankind's greatest invention since Tim Berners-Lee invented the world wide web back in 1989.

You see, although Bitcoin and cryptocurrency in general is a large part of the blockchain movement, it goes beyond that.

There are serious political, social and economic ramifications that will come as a result of decentralization. An incorruptible permanent record, accessible by the masses, has a myriad of uses that can undoubtedly benefit society as a whole.

If you're reading this book, you're mostly likely a skeptic of big government, and you have every right to be. As recently as 2016, we witnessed a United States General Election in which both sides accused the other of vote tampering, in what is supposedly the world's leading democracy.

In short, governance as we know it has to be questioned.

Blockchain technology allows for indisputable trust on a level such as this. Banks, governments, hospitals, all the way down to small one-man-operation businesses can benefit.

That is the true future of this technology.

I hope this is just the start of your blockchain journey, and I hope it not only makes you a lot of money, I hope it enriches the quality of your life.

One final thing, if you enjoy this book I'd appreciate it if you took 2 minutes to leave it a review on Amazon.

Thanks,

Stephen

Chapter 1: What is Blockchain Technology?

Over the past few years, you have likely heard more and more people talking about cryptocurrency this, or blockchain that. If you don't understand these terms, don't worry, you aren't alone. It may be time to jump on the bandwagon, however, as blockchain use is rapidly approaching consumer status with IBM estimating that 15 percent of banks will already be using blockchain technology by the end of 2017.

Simply put, blockchain is the foundation that makes technologies like cryptocurrency possible. On a fundamental level, a blockchain takes data, primarily of financial nature for now, and replicates that data across a vast number of decentralized nodes that could conceivably be spread around the entire world. This process is run not by a centralized network or body, but by a peer-to-peer approach that uses cryptography and digital signatures to keep things running smoothly.

Each new block in a chain contains information regarding various transactions, and possibly what are known as smart contracts, as well as information that links it to the blocks around it. Each block is also timestamped which helps the chain determine its place in the whole thing. The transactions in individual blocks are verified by block miners, third parties who are paid for their work, and are only then added to the chain as a whole.

What miners are actually doing is solving what are known as proof-of-work systems which means they are solving complicated mathematical equations using specialized equipment designed for doing so. The equations prevent security breaches through denial of service attacks and keep things running smoothly. The amount of reward for this type of work varies based on the cryptocurrency that is being mined, as well as the number of people working to complete the block they were chosen to mine. Most cryptocurrencies also charge a small transaction fee, and a part of that fee goes to the miners as well.

Despite the fact that the database information is spread around the world with no central authority, and the fact that sections of it are inspected by third parties on a regular basis, the data that is stored in a blockchain remains incredibly secure. This level of security doesn't come from an active offense against fraud, it comes from the defensive capabilities of the way in which the blockchain is constructed.

If a specific transaction that is being transferred from a node doesn't match up with what the other nodes are saying then that block is discarded in favor of a more accurate one. Essentially, for a false block to make it past the blockchain's defenses, it would need to show up on 51 percent of all of the nodes in the system at the same time. The difficulty of such a task means that it could be done, but the costs involved would more than outweigh the potential reward for doing so.

History lesson

In order to understand the true importance of blockchain technology, it is helpful to understand a little bit about its history. In 2008, a person or a group of persons using the alias Satoshi Nakamoto put forth a whitepaper on the idea of a digital currency that would allow individuals to transfer money to one another in a largely anonymous fashion. This paper, titled, *bitcoin: A Peer-to Peer Electronic Cash System,* was soon followed by the original blockchain and bitcoin code from the same alias. The code was released in an open source fashion, and the Nakamoto name faded from sight as other developers began working on the code in earnest.

The Nakamoto alias was also the first person to distribute bitcoins and then verify the transaction, receiving 50 bitcoins for doing so. For those who are considering investing in a cryptocurrency based on blockchain technology, take note, as the first use of those bitcoins was to trade 10,000 of them for a pair of large pizzas which made each worth about $.002. If you weren't aware, they are doing a little better than that these days with each bitcoin being worth nearly $5,000 as of September 2017.

By 2014, blockchain usage was gaining some traction and a new and improved version of the original code now allowed for entire programs to be contained in blocks along with data that make it possible for a wide variety of tasks to be carried out from within the blockchain. In 2016, the Russian Federation started working on a blockchain program as a means of collecting royalties for copyrighted material, making Russia the first country to official announce a blockchain project, though since that time a number of other countries, including China and the US, have indicated they are working on blockchain projects of their own. When the project was announced, the Russian Economic Minister was quoted as saying that blockchain technology was likely the most important new technology since the invention of the internet.

Over the past few years, another blockchain based company, the Ethereum platform has been gaining a lot of support due to its wide variety of enhanced capabilities when compared to the bitcoin blockchain. The Ethereum platform has its own official cryptocurrency, ether (although the two terms are used interchanably by many commentators), and is also home to an ecosystem of other cryptocurrencies that other programmers have made to run in its framework. It is also home to a wide variety of smart contracts and apps that run on "gas", which is essentially a transaction fee the platform collects for each transaction. Ether blocks that are mind tend to be completed in a shorter timeframe than bitcoin blocks and the Ethereum chain can handle a great many more blocks at a time when compared to the bitcoin chain.

Database differences: The biggest difference between a blockchain database and a traditional database is the level of centralization that is required in order for it to run effectively. Even if a traditional server is decentralized, the core components are going to be arranged as close to one another as possible to facilitate the transfer of information. Instead, blockchains are formed of nodes that are separated by thousands of miles, each communicating with the others through a best use model that means they naturally seek out the nodes that are closest to them and the information spreads out from there.

The fact that mass collaboration and the blockchain code results in a reliable means by which funds can be transferred is a game changer. Blockchain is the first innately digital medium where value can be transferred, in much the way the internet allowed for information to be transmitted digitally.

Hashes: A hash is a mathematical function that makes up a crucial part of the blockchain security matrix. This is the function that ensures the data that is added to a blockchain remains secure regardless of who might get their hands on it. The function encrypts the data in such a way that it becomes a fixed length output, which can be thought of as a type of digital fingerprint. When it comes to blockchain security the most commonly used hash function is SHA-256. SHA-256 is used by cryptocurrencies such as Bitcoin, Omni and Zetacoin.

The hash function for every block is going to be different, which means that if that data is altered by a malevolent third party then the entire fingerprint would be rearranged in unpredictable ways. Additional hash information is added once the block is added to the chain as a whole. This process is repeated throughout the blockchain each time a new block is added so that it is always changing.

Merkle trees: Hashes are then used by a process known as the Merkle tree which is a quick and easy way for the blockchain to verify all of its data once a new block has been added. Each hash is unique and created based on the data it contains which means the Merkle tree then essentially needs to scan the hash, compare it to the root hashes which is the ultimate collection of all the hashes, and then determine if everything lines up as it should. Each time it does this, it creates a pair of roots, one where the data is correct and one where it is not, this way it keeps the core details of the blockchain intact against malicious changes.

Chapter 2: Practical Application of Blockchain Technology

As blockchain technology continues to grow in popularity, the ways in which it can be put to use are growing as well. What follows are a number of different ways blockchain technology is sure to change how business is conducted, day to day life, outside the realm of cryptocurrency and how governments and lawmakers interact with the public.

Business uses

Money transfers and payments: While blockchain technology is already synonymous with cryptocurrency payments, the fact of the matter is that more can be done in that space to facilitate the needs of businesses when it comes to utilizing blockchain to its fullest potential. The Ethereum Enterprise Alliance is a group of major corporations such as Microsoft, JP Morgan and Samsung that are working together to build a blockchain that is based on Ethereum technology but also contains the level of control that businesses would need in order to use the technology on a regular basis.

This type of service, while extremely common in some parts of the world, are extremely hard to come by in others. As such, more people in Kenya currently have a bitcoin wallet than have indoor plumbing. Connecting all these new individuals to the internet is going to have serious positive ramifications for retailers worldwide.

Notary services: Blockchain technology is constructed in such a way that it could conceivably be used to replace traditional notary services. There are already numerous different apps available that allow for notarization of a variety of different types of content.

Cloud storage: Blockchain technology is already being used as a means of connecting users with cloud storage space in an Airbnb like setup. Using this system those with spare storage space on their hard drives can rent out the extra space to those who are in need of extra storage. The estimate is that worldwide spending has reached more than $20 billion for cloud storage so this could be a profitable opportunity if this catches on.

Fraud: Blockchain technology has the potential to increase the efficacy of tracking identities online in a way that is both efficient and secure. Blockchain is uniquely situated to solve this problem because its results are sure to be properly authenticated, immutable, secure and irrefutable. This improved system will do away with complicated password or dual factor authentication systems in favor of a system that will ultimately use digital signatures and cryptography to keep everyone safe and efficiently catalogued.

Using this type of system, the transaction will be processed as normal, and the only check that will be required is if the account from which the funds are drawn, matches the account of the person who authorized the transaction. A variation of this same usage of the technology can also be used when it comes to birth certificates, passports, residency forms, account logins and physical identification. There are already apps available that utilize a blockchain to verify the identity of users from a mobile device.

Supply chain communication: If it is one thing that companies have a hard time dealing with, it is the extreme level of communication that is required in order to ensure that they have all the requirements at the ready to ensure they are ready to do whatever it is they do. Blockchain technology allows for companies to easily track products from door to door, with the internet of things (the ability for everyday objects to send and receive data) connecting shipping containers to accounts that get a steady stream of details about the product in question as it crosses various thresholds and ultimately automatically pays for the goods once they have reached their final location. SkuChain and Provenance are two companies that are working to create these types of systems.

Gift cards: Gift cards are a good idea in theory that ultimately falls apart in practice when it comes time for the customer to actually hold onto the card in question. Blockchain technology has the potential to change all that by connecting customer loyalty products directly to a blockchain which can then verify and update relevant information as needed. Gyft Block is a company that already has a digital gift card up and running on the bitcoin blockchain that can be traded just like a cryptocurrency.

Internet of things: Samsung and IBM are currently working together on a concept referred to as the Autonomous Decentralized Peer-to-Peer Telemetry or ADEPT, which uses blockchain as a means of creating a system that mixes proof of stake and proof of work systems to better secure transactions. Essentially, what they are trying to do is to create a blockchain that would act like a public ledger for a wide number of devices. This public ledger would then serve as a hub which can create a bridge between devices for a very low cost. These devices could then communicate with one another in a practically autonomous fashion, making it easy to save energy, sort out bugs and issue updates.

Insurance contracts: Smart contracts have the possibility to reinvent insurance in a big way. Rather than deal with insurance agents who have to determine liability in case of a business-related injury, a blockchain would be able to make use of a smart contract that issues payments if a specific interconnected item registers a faulty signal. Blockchain would then allow for a more streamlined claim process that would improve the customer experience and ultimately save the company money.

Funding: 4G Capital is a company that provides access to credit for small businesses in Africa through the use of a decentralized app that is running off of the Ethereum blockchain. Donors are able to use the app to spend their cryptocurrency funds directly to the recipient of their choice. The money is then converted to the currency of the applicant and dispersed using a proprietary transaction system. In addition to providing 100 percent unsecured loans to those who often would not be able to get them otherwise, it also provides business training and consulting services. While currently operating in a limited capacity, if it proves successful more operations offering this type of funding are sure to appear.

Microblogging: Businesses are always looking for new ways to interact with their target audience and blockchain may be the next new frontier. Projects like Eth-Tweet offer decentralized microblogging services through the Ethereum blockchain. The service operates much like Twitter, except that as a truly decentralized entity there is no one who can pressure users to take content down and no one can remove messages after they have been added to the chain.

Day to Day Life

Healthcare: Real world tests are already being done that link individuals to their healthcare status as they are going through a hospital. Early studies from the MIT Media Lab show that this practice can decrease errors by up to 30 percent in nonemergency situations. This is a huge step forward for hospitals that are often not designed for the volume and range of data that is being created these days. Patient data can even continue to be gathered on an outpatient basis or if the individual has agreed to be part of a test group. Payment for these tests could then be issued automatically once the required data has been successfully gathered.

Internet decentralization: With the rise of Google, the internet is a much more centralized place than it once was. A startup by the name of Blockstack is working to change all of that. It is on track to release prototype software in the second half of 2017 which will make it possible for anyone to utilize blockchain technology to access a version of the internet where you have much more control over your personal data. This decentralized internet will act the same way the traditional internet does, except that instead of creating a different account for every website, the process will reverse and you will create a primary account, then give certain sites access to it.

If you are then finished using a specific site you can then completely revoke its access to your data at any time. While this might seem like a small step, it is actually a giant leap for a new and improved internet. Blockstack makes use of a digital ledger to track usernames and various levels of encryption, with the end result being a greater degree of privacy control for the individual user. The blockchain will also keep track of domain names as well, potentially making ICANN, the web domain oversight body, obsolete. Microsoft is already in talks with Blockstack to make use of its technology.

While the way it handles web functions might seem extreme, it is actually the low-level features of the internet as a whole that have led to the dominance of corporations who essentially have free reign to treat user data as they see fit. The new platform will still offer companies ways to make money while providing services, the balance of power is just going to favor the consumer more than it does now.

Improved property rights: Both tangible and intangible property from cars and houses on one hand to company shares and patents on the other, can all be connected via smart contract and blockchain technology to make determining the rights to these items much less complicated than it currently is. These details could be stored in a type of decentralized ledger along with related contractual details regarding the true ownership of the property in question. The technology could even extend to smart keys which could then give specific users access to specific property.

The ledger would keep track of the finer details and activate specific keys as needed. In this case the decentralized ledger is also a system for managing and recording property rights and also creating duplicates if smart keys are lost. Implementing smart property protocols will help to decrease the average property owner's risk of fraud, questionable business deals and mediation fees.

New types of money lenders: With blockchain technology making it easier and easier to transfer funds between individuals, new types of hard money lenders are already popping up to take advantage of the fact. Hard money lenders are more likely to offer terms to individuals who already have subpar credit, unfortunately the terms are often quite high and often property is listed as collateral. This, in turn, causes many debtors to default on loans, and leaves them in a worse position than they were in initially. Lending via blockchain technology has the potential to change all of that as the binding nature of the transaction means that less collateral will be required and smart contracts can take care of the transactions themselves so costs will be decreased as well.

Smarter smartphones: Smartphones already operate on a type of cryptography in that they require either your fingerprint, a scan of your face, or a password in order to activate them. This is already a form of smart property, just in its nascent stages. This facet of personal technology will be enhanced via blockchain technology in that, rather than having these details tied to your physical SIM card, they will be stored in the blockchain where you can easily access them no matter where you are. While issues concerning security would typically arise in these sorts of situations, the fact that each transaction needs to be verified in order to add it to the chain ensures security remains tight.

Passports: Blockchains have been helping people manage their passports since at least 2014 by making it easier for users to identify themselves regardless if they are online or offline. This system works by taking a picture of the user and encoding it with a private key as well as a public one. The passport is then stored in a public ledger which can be accessed via a blockchain address by the person who has the key.

Important documents: It doesn't matter if it is a wedding certificate, birth certificate or death certificate, all of these documents confer various rights or privileges. This would be less of an issue if it weren't for the fact that the physical systems that keep track of these details are prone to mistakes. In fact, according to UNICEF, as many as 30 percent of all children who are below the age of five do not have a birth certificate. Implementing a public blockchain to streamline this process would not only make keeping track of these services more manageable, it will make these documents easier to obtain as well.

Identification: Currently you have to carry your driver's license, your work identification card, your social security card, the list goes on and on. With the right blockchain, however, all of this could be a thing of the past. Eventually everyone is going to have a digital ID that goes with them everywhere. It will be connected to a worldwide protected ledger and it will contain all the basic details you now need to carry around with you.

Improve digital interactions: With a wider and wider variety of interactions being initiated online, it is often difficult to know whom you can trust. Blockchain can alleviate that problem by storing a version of your identity in a blockchain that is available for everyone to see. It would automatically pull in things like review scores and rankings from a wide variety of sites so you always have at least a general idea of what you are in for before taking an online interaction into the real world. Unlike with more traditional types of social media, users would not have the ability to remove their information and start fresh, once it is in the blockchain it would be there forever.

Change the way you fuel your vehicle: Modern electric vehicles have already made great strides when it comes to the fueling process. Another important stride is on the horizon and it has to do with blockchain. Soon blockchain technology will be able to track the electricity that a given owner uses and automatically deduct the funds from the relevant account. All the owner would need to do is pull up to the charging station, the blockchain will take care of the rest.

Beyond Cryptocurrency

Fund HIV research: The UBS bank recently donated a platform to Finclusion systems that will launch a smart contract called HealBond which will seek out efficient trades on the bonds market so that the funds that it makes can ultimately be put to use for HIV research. Analysts are confident that with the right level of passive strategy it could start making money right away. If this proves successful then it will give those with the resources to do so even more ways to help out their favorite causes.

Data security: The company Factom is turning its focus to properly securing data. Currently it is working with the country of Honduras to more accurately register land and also with a number of cities in China on what are known as Smart Cities. Blockchain technology is looking to an integral tool in getting all the various different systems communicating with one another on the same level. This includes things like data notarization services as well as information management with a much higher level of integrity than what is currently available to the public. Factom has also already received funding from the US Department of Homeland Security, specifically the Technology and Science Directorate to work on the Blockchain Software to Prove Integrity of Captured Data project.

Decentralize the power grid: Rather than requiring a centralized power provider that is in charge of sending energy to workplaces and homes, a decentralized blockchain could be built to allow people to generate power through solar and other means and then sell what they don't need on an open market. All of these transactions would then be visible on the blockchain, keeping fraud to a minimum. As more and more individuals are purchasing high-capacity batteries along with solar panels for their rooftops, this type of scenario is fast becoming a realistic possibility.

Track things that are difficult to track: The fact that a blockchain can show up at any time and cannot be altered makes it uniquely qualified to track the types of items that always seem to go missing. For example, the company Everledger is currently working on a way to identify specific objects and then determine whether or not they are legitimate. So far, they have created a distributed ledger that follows various diamond transaction verifications including law enforcement agencies, claimants, insurance companies and owners to put together a mine to store view of each diamond. The system is useful in that it keeps the supply chain honest and also makes it easier for individual buyers to determine if a given diamond is right for them. Furthermore, smart contracts make it possible for the diamond transactions to clearly be paid for while also tracking them, guaranteeing to consumers that they are not purchasing blood diamonds.

Getting artists what they deserve: Rather than having to worry about making sure their music isn't used without generating compensation, with blockchain, musicians will soon be able to determine who used each song and for what, with each individual transaction being carried out via smart contracts through a blockchain platform. What's more, rather than having to wait for funds to hit a specific level, or for someone, somewhere, to cut a check, these funds would be distributed in relatively real time. This same process can be applied to music licensing as a whole which means it will eventually be possible to cut out middlemen from the equation entirely. This, in turn, means a decrease in costs to the consumer and an increase in profit for the musicians as it means people are more likely to pay for content again.

Improved communication: Currently if your vehicle receives a safety recall then the maker of the vehicle sends out a notice to all of its licensed sales outlets and each of these outlets then reaches out to its customers who have purchased the vehicle in question. This information then may or may not reach you, allowing you to then make an informed decision based on the details you have available to you. The recall could be for something major, or something inconsequential, but regardless you are certainly going to want to know about it. Placing all of this information onto a blockchain would dramatically simplify the process as after the defect was found, the chain could automatically notify the owners in question.

Clarifying asset lifecycles: It doesn't matter who you are or what you do, you have certain tools that make your life possible. Blockchain technology has the ability to make sure you know as much about them as you need to when combined with the internet of things. Asset lifecycle is important for everyone from home business owners to multinational corporations, and the information provided by this type of blockchain could literally save lives. For example, think about an airplane which is likely to have several different owners during its time in the air. This type of blockchain would make it possible for every owner to understand every part on their airplane more completely and to ensure that proper maintenance has been completed throughout its lifetime.

Tracking the food chain: An increase in the ready availability of blockchain technology means that slowly but surely concerns about the quality of the food that you consume on a regular basis will be put to rest. Regardless of the final state of the product when you purchase it, you should be able to see the entire route it took to get to your table. Not just the completed product either, everything that went into the construction of the completed whole. This is particularly useful as there may be more to the traditional food chain than you might first realize. For example, a farm could produce vegetables that head to a processing facility before ending up in a distribution center before being purchased and run through another processing facility, all to end up in a can of tomato soup.

Change the value of ownership: The company Slock.it is based on the Ethereum platform and runs a blockchain for what is known as the Universal Share Network, this network is an opensource marketplace where anyone can go to list their unused asset, regardless if it is machinery, shipping containers, office space and more. It is a sort of automated AirBnB that works for anything and everything, not just temporary living arrangements. The fundamentals of blockchain technology are then passed on to tangible, real world assets.

Transportation: A variation in the trend towards the crowdsourcing of ridesharing applications, La'Zooz is a decentralized transportation platform that is owned by its users who use blockchain technology to organize and optimize a variety of smart transportation solutions.

Government and lawmakers

Everywhere around the world, government organizations are rapidly exploring the many possibilities provided by blockchain and distributed ledger technology. The ability to suddenly be able to record and distribute ledger information easily and securely has created a market for a variety of new governmental approaches when it comes to establishing trust, preventing fraud and improving transparency.

From a recent survey from the Economic Intelligence Unit as well as IBM, it is clear that the interest in blockchain technology from various worldwide governments is quite high. In fact, as many as 9 out of 10 government agencies are already planning on investing in blockchain based contract management, asset management, regulatory compliance and transaction management by 2018. Meanwhile 7 of the 10 predict blockchain is going to significantly change the way that contract management is handled. Finally, nearly 20 percent say that they expect to have a blockchain plan up and running before the end of 2017.

Voting: As recently as the 2016 United States general election, both Republicans and Democrats could be heard questioning the security of the existing voting system. Likewise, the 2000 presidential election proved that the way that votes are tallied is remarkably out of date. While concerns about hacking have limited the acceptance of electronic means of voting so far, blockchain technology could easily put those fears to rest. A decentralized public ledger would naturally be encrypted but specific individuals could still confirm their votes were counted accurately. This system would not only be more efficient, but it would be more cost effective, and clearly more secure as well.

Responsive, open data: The blockchain ledger would also create a platform for what is known as responsive, open data. Studies show that this type of freely accessible data is likely to bring in nearly $3 trillion worldwide within the first year. Startups will be able to utilize this data to help get ahead of fraudulent activity, parents would be able to access details about the medications their children are receiving, the list is literally endless. Currently, this type of data is only available via limited, government approved windows which are not designed to put citizens first. As a blockchain is a type of public ledger, citizens would be able to access its data at any time and place.

Self-management: Blockchain provides the opportunity for governmental agencies to self-manage more easily as the exchange of information on a global scale would be greatly improved overall. There would be a great deal more trust as well because the information in the blockchain would be public for everyone to see.

Reducing administration costs: If property records were recorded to a blockchain then prospective buyers could more easily, quickly and cost effectively verify ownership information. This process is currently still done manually which means government agencies spend hundreds of thousands of dollars per year paying individuals who do this type of job. Manually verifying such things can also lead to an increased number of errors which helps to further increase potential costs.

It would also greatly decrease the amount of manual effort which would be required on the banks' end as they would have to do much less work when it comes to title insurance. Title insurance is required by lenders as a means to protect their interests. This, in turn, would decrease prices for homebuyers who are refinancing or buying for the first time because they would have to pay less throughout the entire process as the amount of labor would be reduced significantly.

Decrease money laundering: If identity data was readily store on a blockchain, the government agencies could more easily keep track of those who are moving large amounts of money from one place to another. Financial organizations could scan the details of every new client and that information could then be passed along to appropriate agencies if a need presented itself. Furthermore, storing payment and account information in a blockchain would go a long way to standardize the type of information required for an account. This, in turn, will help to improve the quality of the data that is gathered and reduce the number of legitimate transactions that are falsely listed as fraudulent. Finally, having a record that was known to be tamper-proof would make it easier for these organizations to comply with AML regulations.

Ensuring taxpayers are paying up: The Federal Government is likely already working on its own form of cryptocurrency, so there is no reason to assume they are not already working on a means of linking a blockchain to the current IRS system. This blockchain would not only record the amount of money each citizen earned in a year but also any incentives, subsidies, grants and loans that individual might have been provided with as well as there original source. While this will likely lead to more individuals having to pay more in taxes than they are currently, it will also keep the government accountable for every dime that they bring in. It will be much more difficult for money to disappear into the folds of bureaucratic pockets when a blockchain that anyone can see is keeping track of the tab.

Keeping track of incorporated company details: The state of Delaware marks the first state in the nation offer incorporated businesses the ability to keep track of their shareholder rights as well as their equity via blockchain. As it is common for many companies to incorporate in Delaware to take advantage of friendly taxation privileges, this has the potential to be a change that has wide-ranging results. The state is also moving its archival records onto a distributed ledger, so that more people can view it, for free, at less cost to taxpayers.

Digital proof of residency: In Estonia, long known for its forward-thinking practices, it is now possible to digitally apply for residency in the country through the use of a governmental blockchain. New residents then receive a digital key card that corresponds to a cryptographic key that can be used to sign secure documents, taking the place of any signatures on official paperwork. Virtual residents are then free to open up bank accounts in Estonia's online banking system, which also utilizes blockchain, as well as incorporate a company or access other e-services. Estonia is proud to be pushing the boundaries of digital transactions and seeing a variety of new monetary streams in the process.

Welfare: In the United Kingdom, blockchain has already been turned into a service that is available to purchase through the Digital Marketplace run by the government. Through this service, various governmental agencies freely experiment, deploy and build digital services based on blockchain and technology based on distributed ledgers. Last year they ran a trial through the Department for Work and Pension that allowed users to take advantage of a mobile app that let them access their monthly benefit payments along with transferring details to a separate distributed ledger as a means of helping them with managing their finances, with their consent of course.

Global Blockchain Council: The Global Blockchain Council has been set up in Dubai and represents more than 50 public and private organizations that have already launched proof-of-concept blockchain projects across the shipping, tourism, digital wills, business registration, title transfer, healthcare records and diamond trading sectors. IBM has also partnered with the organization in hopes of using its blockchain for a logistics and trade solution. The government of Dubai has also announced plans for an initiative to transfer all of their government documents onto an interconnected blockchain by 2020. The estimated cost reduction from this program is anticipated to be at 25.1 million-man hours per year.

The future of blockchain

While blockchain technology is still in a nascent enough stage that virtually anything can happen, there are a number of things that are being worked on at a governmental level that should be consider in the context of your future usage.

More control: As previously mentioned, one of the biggest benefits of a blockchain is its ability to function completely autonomously. However, due to the fact that bitcoin then allowed for near-anonymous transactions, it made it very easy for those with an interest in avoiding the law to do so. As cryptocurrency becomes more well-known, regulatory and governmental agencies including the Securities and Exchange Commission, Department of Homeland Security, FBI, and the Financial Crimes Enforcement Network, just in the US, have all started becoming more interested in its potential for unlawful activities.

Scrutiny began to increase during 2013 when the Financial Crimes Enforcement Network decided that cryptocurrency exchanges represented a form of an existing money service business. This meant that they would then fall under government regulations. DHS quickly took advantage of this fact to freeze the accounts of Mt. Gox, the biggest bitcoin exchange in the world at this time based on accusations of money laundering.

This was then followed up with a more recent SEC ruling to deny bitcoin the ability to open an official cryptocurrency exchange trade fund. This move led to a decrease in the price of bitcoin, though that decrease was then countered by an even stronger increase. The denial of this application was still pending review as of September 2017. This then places cryptocurrencies into a bit of an odd situation as their increasing levels of scrutiny makes it harder for them to follow through on their purpose, despite being more popular than ever.

If cryptocurrency is every going to reach a truly mainstream level, and be absorbed into existing financial systems then it needs to find a way to remain true to its initial purpose while also becoming complex enough to hold off the security threats it is sure to face in the future. What's more, it will also need to become simple enough that the average person can use it without issue. Finally, it would need to remain decentralized enough to still be recognizable, while also including various checks and balances to prevent misuse when it comes to things like money laundering or tax evasion. Taken together, this makes it likely that the successful blockchain of the future is going to be some sort of amalgamation of the current form and a more traditional currency.

United States: The United States government is currently working hard to crack down on those who are using blockchain as a means to launder money. They aren't going to be content with that level of control for long, it seems, as signs point to the fact that they are currently working on their own blockchain based cryptocurrency known as Fedcoin. The idea here is that the Federal Reserve could generate a unique cryptocurrency quite easily. The only difference between the blockchain they create and any other is the fact that it would allow for the Federal Reserve to retain the power to go in an remove transactions that they don't approve of.

The rollout of the Fedcoin would occur after the genesis block were created and the rate of Fedcoins being set to 1 to 1 with the dollar. Over time, it would become more and more difficult to come across regular dollars until they were phased out entirely. This would then ultimately lead to a type of cryptocurrency that is both decentralized for its individual transactions, and centralized when it comes to things like limiting available supply and keeping an eye on all types of transactions.

The Federal Reserve is already on its way towards making this plan a reality, so much so that they hosted a closed-door meeting with bitcoin authorities in the fall of 2016. The Chair of the Federal Reserve sat in on the meeting in person, along with representatives from the Bank for International Settlements, World Bank and the International Monetary Fund. During this meeting, one of the talks was literally titled Why Central Banks Will Issue Digital Currencies.

Russia: Russia issued a dramatic shift in its cryptocurrency polices in 2017. Prior to this point anyone caught using cryptocurrency could face jail time, now however the country is embracing digital currency wholeheartedly. The reason for this is related to the extreme level of corruption that Russia has seen in its banking sector over the past several years. More than one hundred banks have been closed in the past three years, and a rash of money laundering schemes still can't be stopped.

To better track where its money is going, the Russian government is currently working on several blockchain based technical applications that will make it easier for them to monitor real time transactions. This makes it appear as though they are less interested in creating a new digital currency and are instead more interested in the distributed ledger portion of the blockchain technology. There is currently no word yet on if Russia plans to create a new blockchain or utilize an existing blockchain for its own ends.

China: China is currently a major supporter in the blockchain space. In June of 2017, the People's Bank of China released and official news report regarding the creation of its own type of digital currency with the ability to scale dramatically depending on the number of transactions that are seen per day. While all of the details have not yet been released, various sources seem to indicate that the bank could release the currency to the world alongside its renminbi project. While no firm release date is forthcoming, the currency is already well underway in the development process and has already seeing testing amongst many of the country's commercial banks and the People's Bank. This testing is a huge step forward for officially sanctioned cryptocurrencies and blockchains of all types. It also proves how committed China is to the idea of thoroughly exploring the digital currency space.

The digital currency they are creating is likely to cause major gains for their economy overall. This is due to the fact that it is back by the People's Bank which means it is functionally the same as a bank note with far fewer associated fees. It would also do a good deal when it comes to bringing banking in China to the modern age as many of its citizens do not have access to traditional banking services.

Chapter 3: Cryptocurrency and Blockchain Interactions

While blockchain is poised to do a great many different things in the near future, for now the most important thing you are going to want to keep in mind is that blockchains make cryptocurrency possible, and bitcoin jumped in price more than $2,000 during the summer of 2017. While this price has pushed it out of the league of many amateur investors, there are more than 1,000 different cryptocurrencies on the market these days so there are plenty of opportunities out there for those who are interested in a potentially profitable investment. This is not to say that there isn't risk involved as well, however, so it is important to keep the risks of cryptocurrency investment in mind as well before making any investments in the space.

Pros

Lowers risk of identity theft: As cryptocurrencies are purely digital, they are naturally susceptible to far less risk than traditional types of currency. They cannot be forged or counterfeited and the transaction cannot be manipulated so that it never happened do to the underlying blockchain. Additionally, once you have bought into a cryptocurrency you can move it about freely without have to worry about transactions with specious companies or individuals putting your details in places they would rather not be. Instead, with most exchanges if you already own cryptocurrency there is no type of verification whatsoever. With most exchanges, without cryptocurrency in hand, you need to generate a new debit or credit transaction with each round of funding.

Easy access: There are roughly 3.5 billion people who have some type of internet access and also do not have any reliable form of banking. This is a niche that the cryptocurrency market is looking to take advantage of to the fullest, and is expected to cause significant growth in the industry as it becomes more commonplace. Assuming this type of banking catches on, then those who invest in cryptocurrency early are going to see more than just a profit, they could potentially see profit on a significant scale.

Low cost: While every cryptocurrency interaction involves a transaction fee, the fees for making this type of exchange is still generally lower than making an exchange on a traditional broker website.

Cons

New technology: While bitcoin has been a quality investment for the past few years, the cryptocurrency market as a whole is still extremely untested overall which means that many of its risks are still very poorly defined, especially when compared to more traditional markets. This naturally makes the highs in the market more dramatic than similar markets, but it also makes the lowers much more dramatic as well. There are no guarantees when one is going to become the other, trends can come and go in completely unpredictable patterns that no one has seen before. What it all comes down to is that there just is not enough information available to be able to accurately predict where the market is going to be in a year, much less five. Until the market stabilizes somewhat, there is no way of telling if every dollar you invest is going to be worth $2, one year from now or if it is going to be worth $.02.

Extreme volatility: Bitcoin, the most stable of all of the cryptocurrencies, is still five time more volatile than gold and has nearly seven times more volatility than if you were to invest that money into the S&P 500. While volatility means a greater chance at profit, it also means the chance at a loss is going to be much higher than it would otherwise be. It is also important to understand that most of the purchases of cryptocurrency that are made, are done for speculative purposes. This means that the currency is being purchased by investors, not people who are actually planning to use it on a day-to-day basis. This, in turn means that prices are likely to rise higher than a true supply and demand market would indicate. This early adopter phenomenon means those who buy in early are going to experience a nice price increase, but the upward movement ultimately won't last. This isn't a question of if, it is a question of when.

Lack of physicality: While the fact that cryptocurrency is a digital means of payment is one of its leading characteristics, the fact remains that this concept does present some challenges. Specifically, consider the fact that if the server holding your cryptocurrency goes down, and there is no backup, then your investment is gone forever. You can take a variety of methods to put the control of your cryptocurrency in your hands, but the fact remains that a real coin is always going to be easier to hold onto than a digital one.

The vast potential for profit when it comes to hacking into a blockchain also means that hackers are never going to stop trying to do just that. What this also means, is that they are occasionally going to be successful. For example, the Ethereum platform has seen a variety of different attacks throughout its lifetime, one of which was so successful that it necessitated a hard fork that saw the Ethereum blockchain divided into those that saw a profit from the attack and those who lost out because of it. A split in the value of the dollar is never going to occur, no matter how many are stolen in a bank robbery which just proves how unpredictable investing in a new opportunity can be.

Trading cryptocurrency

Regardless of how familiar you are with trading traditional securities, trading in the cryptocurrency market can prove to be extremely profitable, as long as you have come to terms with the potential for risk. Don't forget, it is important to never invest any money that you can't afford to lose. There is very little barrier to entry, as previously mentioned, if you already have cryptocurrency then you won't even need to worry about verifying your account.

Another useful thing about trading in this market is the fact that there are no centralized exchanges which means it is every exchange for itself. This then leads to a market that is very fragmented, which means it naturally produces spreads that are much wider than you are likely to see anywhere else. This lack of regulation also means it is often quite easy to find a very large margin which means that small investments have the potential to become large returns faster than with virtually all other types of investment, though the same can be said about losses as well. Finally, depending on the cryptocurrency you are trading in, you will likely be able to find it for different rates on different exchanges which means you might be able to make a profit simply by purchasing them in one place and selling them somewhere else.

The most common way to trade cryptocurrencies through a trading company is with a contract for differences. This type of contract binds the buyer and seller together for the length of the contract, once it ends, the buyer will pay the seller the difference between the price of the asset at the end of the contract and what it was at the start. If the price moves the other way then the seller has to pay the buyer the difference. When it comes to securing leverage, you will likely be able to find rates in excess of 20 to 1, though it is not recommended that you seek them out until you are very familiar with what it is like to trade in this market.

Global currency: When it comes to standard currency, the number of things that can influence the price is naturally going to be fairly limited. The opposite is true for cryptocurrencies, however, and it is difficult to tell what is going to set investors off before it happens. Any currency news anywhere has the potential to set prices shifting dramatically, in fact, several of bitcoin's most significant moves have come about due to the introduction to controls for capital in Greece and when China devalued the Yuan.

Market always ready: While the forex market is traditionally thought of as the most robust market as it is open 120 hours each week, the cryptocurrency market is open 168 hours each week, and trades are always happening regardless of what part of the world is currently active. Currently there are about 100 major cryptocurrency exchanges in the world who all offer various levels of trading along with differing rates based on their level of service. As such, it should not take more than a little research to find the one that is right for you.

This can also be seen as a negative, depending on your tolerance for risk as these factors can be enough to generate large swings on a daily basis. In fact, price shifts of more than 5 percent are common on most days for the larger cryptocurrencies and the smaller ones aren't surprised if they see 15 percent movement or more.

Finding your exchange

When it comes to committing to a specific exchange, it is important to always do the relevant research that you need in order to feel comfortable about your choice. Moving forward without doing enough research can cause you to end up in a situation where you exchange suddenly disappears with your money or you find out that it doesn't have the funds to cover all of its obligations and there is a run on it as everyone tries to get their money back at once. If this sort of thing were to happen, it is important to keep in mind that you are going to have very little recourse, especially if you choose an exchange that is not based in your country. This is why the initial choice you make has the potential to be so impactful.

Prioritize transparent exchanges: As a general rule, the more transparent the exchange you choose is willing to be, the more on the level it is going to be. This means you are going to want to be able to take a look at their order book, which is just a version of their distributed ledger and shows how much of everything is being bought or sold on a regular basis. You should also be able to request details regarding where their funds are held and their system for verifying their appropriate level of reserve currency. If you have a hard time getting answers to these very basic questions then the exchange might simply not have the means to make that information public. On the other hand, it could mean that they are a fractional exchange and can't cover their debts. When it comes to choosing the right cryptocurrency exchange it is always better to be safe than sorry.

Available security: It is very important to always choose an exchange with a healthy level of security, after all, as previously mentioned your cryptocurrency profits won't exist outside this exchange without your help which means security is of the upmost importance. You will only want to use exchanges that have an HTTPS in front of their URL as this indicates they are operating off of a secure protocol which means they are actively working to keep your account details from being stolen. You will also want to ensure that the exchange is utilizing a type of two-factor authentication in addition to standard secure login practices. If your exchange isn't at least this well protected then you are flirting with theft of both your identity and your investments.

Fees add up: Almost every type of cryptocurrency has an associated fee that is paid, part of which goes to the blockchain platform holder and part goes to the miner or miners who verify your transaction. While these fees are certainly voluntary, in most cases, not paying them removes much of the incentive for your transaction to be verified which means the entire process might end up taking longer than it otherwise would. Unless you choose an exchange in China, you will then also have to pay a transaction fee to the exchange as well. With so many fees flying around, they can add up quickly which means you are always going to have a trading plan in place before you make your first trade to prevent yourself from losing a sizeable portion of your trading capital to fees.

Try for something local: Despite the fact that there are cryptocurrency exchanges worldwide, you should aim for one that operates in your home country if possible. This is advantageous in multiple ways, the first of which is that you will naturally be able to take advantage of periods of higher volume simply because you will be on the same general time zone as your exchange. Choosing a local option will also make it easier should you ever need to contact support, and your deposits will go through more quickly as well. Even better, depending on your country and its laws, there might even be some type of oversight regarding cryptocurrency exchanges which means getting your money back after some funny business might not be completely out of the question.

When choosing a local exchange, make sure to verify they offer the cryptocurrency pairs that you are looking for. Exchanges vary dramatically from one to the next so there are no guarantees you will even be able to trade in your local currency, even if you pick an exchange that is close to home.

Understand transaction times: As all cryptocurrency transaction need to be verified and added to the blockchain before they can clear, exchanges often work on a bit of a lead time to let this process breathe. It is important that you choose an exchange whose transaction time is reasonable, for the best results. Likewise, you are going to want to ensure that the price you buy at is the price that is locked in regardless of how long the transaction takes. If this is not the case then you risk making a trade that looks promising, only to have the price change and ruin everything before it actually goes through.

Well-known exchanges

Kraken: This is a European exchange that handles the highest volume of euro trades each day. They are also within the top 15 when it comes to USD exchanges as well.

Coinbase: This is the elder statesman of the cryptocurrency exchanges in the US and has the honor of being the oldest continuously active USD exchange. It is known for being strictly regulated and is still one of the top five when it comes to pure volume traded per day.

OKCoin: This is primarily a USD exchange that is based in Japan which means it is subject to far fewer regulations than most of the other exchanges in this list. If you are looking for higher margins and few fees, and are comfortable with the extra risk, then this is the exchange for you.

Bitstamp: This exchange has been running continuously since 2011 and the second most commonly used USD exchange with a volume greater than 10,000 units a day.

Bitfinex: This exchange does the greatest amount of USD trading by volume of all the exchanges, worldwide, clearing more than 200,000 units of cryptocurrency every single week. If you are interested in going with this option, be aware that if you already own cryptocurrency then you can get started without submitting to any type of verification.

Initial coin offerings (ICOs)

In 2017, a blockchain based company managed to raise more than $150 million in less than 24 hours and another, Status.im managed half that amount. These outpourings of investor generosity are known as initial coin offerings and, like everything having to do with cryptocurrency, they offer a heavy risk in exchange for a potentially lucrative reward. As of summer, 2017, the process had already raised nearly $500,000,000.

Despite being a play on the term initial public offering, the initial coin offering is actually a very different beast in almost every way. An initial coin offering is really just another crowdfunding strategy where a blockchain company offers its new cryptocurrency at a very investor-friendly rate and then investors buy it up in hopes of seeing the price rise even as little as 50 cents. The company then, in theory at least, will have the money to complete its project and come to market, where its products or services will be so widely adopted that the price of its cryptocurrency will rise based on increased demand. The Ethereum platform has quickly proven itself the most popular home for companies who are looking to offer an initial coin offering.

A majority of this money currently comes from China, though investors from around the world have been known to open their checkbooks if the price is right. While investing on what is more or less an unknown quantity always comes with certain risks, initial coin offerings are even riskier still. This is due to the fact that they are not currently under the SEC regulatory umbrella which means their business plans are not put through the same testing that those who apply for an initial public offering are. There is also some concern that the success that the first few initial coin offerings garnered is actually due to another bubble which means it is unlikely to last.

While they do have issues, initial coin offerings also have the potential to generate serious profits for investors who make the right decisions at the right times. Nevertheless, if you are considering this type of investment then you need to understand that if you choose to invest in an initial coin offering, then you are making one of the riskiest investments possible.

To counteract the potential danger as much as possible, you will need to approach all initial coin offerings with a quizzical mindset and the first thing you will want to do is look through any information the company has made available including, hopefully, a business plan. This will make it easier for you to determine if a specific project makes sense on a financial level and to ensure that is business proposition checks out in the long-term. You will also need to know that the market is going to actually want the product or service the company is hoping to provide. Furthermore, you will want to double check and see what the role of the cryptocurrency that you are buying into will be when the product or service is up and running.

You will also need to keep in mind that buying into an initial coin offering is going to be quite different than buying into an initial public offering. When buying into the latter, you come away with ownership shares that essentially mean you own a small portion of the company in question. Initial coin offerings grant you no such rights, just a pile of digital currency that may or may not eventually be worth something. Additionally, initial public offerings have stricter requirements placed on them including accreditation obligations and fiduciary requirements that the company must meet before it can have its offering, none of which is required for initial coin offerings.

In reality, you are likely never going to see more than a whitepaper, business plan and website from an initial coin offering company, and sometimes not even all of these. They are more than likely not going to have a product or prototype to show off either which means you are going to be taking a lot of what is being told to you on faith. You also need to be aware that just because an initial coin offering sees a good amount of response early on, doesn't mean this goodwill will last until its launch day, much less beyond it. Also noteworthy is the fact that many analysts believe that giving new companies too much money too soon actually limits their potential as the owner's feel the need to spend all the money available to them while feeling less inclined to actually complete a usable product.

While the list of poor ICOs ranges from those with overly optimistic ideas to downright scams with the sole goal of taking your hard earned cash. There are an increasing number of ICOs out there with nothing more than a flashy website filled with a ton of buzzwords and a high valuation based on nothing more than their own opinion. The single biggest factor you should examine before investing is the real world viability of the project. What solution to a current problem does the company promise to solve? Even more so, is there even a problem in the first place that requires blockchain technology? It's important to examine the team behind the project, and more importantly their previous track record with projects like it. Another main determinant should be whether the token they are offering has actual utility for the project, or are investors just going to dump it for a quick profit as soon as it hits the open market? You should also watch out for any huge bonuses offered for early investors. It's not uncommon for a pre-sale bonus to be offered, but if these bonuses top 100%, you can and should question what the incentive is for non-early adopters, and if the team are just trying to generate as much cash as quickly as possible. One advantage the Ethereum platform does have is the ability for smart contracts to be coded into the ICO, such as funds held in a service similar to escrow, to ensure they are returned to investors if the project founders do not uphold their end of the agreement.

Last but not least, it is worth noting that a majority of the currently successful initial coin offerings have been based on the Ethereum blockchain platform which means the basis of these companies is still essentially an untested technology. While the Ethereum blockchain platform has a better chance of making it than making it than most, the fact of the matter is that it is still untested technology so there is still downside potential as well as upside. Overall, it might be the best choice to instead wait and see how the first round of initial coin offering companies pan out before getting too involved with these types of investments directly.

Tips for investing successfully

While starting to invest in cryptocurrency is as easy as finding an exchange and putting some money into the cryptocurrency machine, doing so and turning an investment profit is something else completely. What's next is a list of things you will want to keep in mind in order to invest successfully in the long-term.

It's a commodity: The first thing you are going to need to do is to think about cryptocurrency in the same way you would any other commodity. Just like any other commodity, cryptocurrency is used for practical as well as investment purposes, just as precious metals have commercial uses and base metals have industrial ones. Additionally, they are all trade through exchanges that more or less all follow the same rules. This means that in order to choose a cryptocurrency that is likely to increase in value, you are going to want to pick the one that is likely to provide the most real-world value or has the greatest number of probable uses beyond just P2P transactions.

Increasing usage: When gathered together as a whole, all the currently existing cryptocurrencies have a market cap of about $160 billion. This puts them in the same league as companies like Tesla and Microsoft in terms of pure numbers. What makes this number particularly interesting is that real world usage and increasing market cap have gone hand in hand so far, and reports show that blockchain and cryptocurrency usage is only likely to increase for at least the next five years.

This is when market saturation is expected to occur and is likely when many of the existing bubbles break for the first time. Nevertheless, while the market is still extremely volatile in the short-term, cryptocurrency as a long-term investment should be relatively reliable. When this number is looked at through the lens of the current market cap then the potential for growth is truly staggering. Essentially the price of cryptocurrency across the board has nowhere to go but up. Even better, once the number of users eventually stabilizes, investor won't have to worry about the bubble effect nearly as much because prices will likely stop decreasing dramatically at that point as well.

Point in the cycle: The market cycle is a type of investment pattern that every investment goes through sooner or later. On the positive side, it starts with optimism before moving up to thrill, and then peaking with euphoria. It then decreases through anxiety, denial, fear, depression and finally, panic. After it bottoms out it then rises back up through depression, hope and relief before once again reaching optimism.

While bitcoin has already been through the cycle more than once, most recently bottoming out during the 2014 crash, the vast majority of all cryptocurrencies are still very much in the optimism stage so there is still plenty of time to get in while the getting is good. As long as you do your research correctly in the first place there is no reason you couldn't realistically see five reliable years of growth on your investment before it hits the euphoria stage.

While this is decidedly good news, it is also important to keep in mind the fact that the cryptocurrency market today, is very much the same as the dotcom boom of the 90s. What this means, is that roughly 80 percent of all the cryptocurrencies on the market today are going to fail before or during the period when the market hits its saturation point. This is due to the fact that there will only be so many options in a limited marketplace that only a handful will be able to survive the buildup. Many investors will end up throwing their money at a company without having any idea what that company actually does and the market will crumble because of it, though if you know what's coming you will be able to avoid the worst of it.

Solving problems is key: It doesn't matter what the potential for profit on a given cryptocurrency turns out to be, buying into it and then sitting back to wait for the magic to happen will never be the most effective money-making strategy. Instead, you will be better served putting time into finding those cryptocurrencies that solve problems for individual markets or, even better, the world at large. The bigger the problem being solved, the more likely it will turn into something that is worth investing in for the long-term. It is especially important to consider solutions when it comes to the banking services that some parts of the world take for granted. Cryptocurrencies that focus on solutions when it comes to making payments and wiring money are going to be good bets in the near future.

Long-term view: Given the amount of movement you can expect to see on a regular basis, the ideal cryptocurrency portfolio is going to be one that focuses solely on the long-term. You are also going to want to make a point of picking several different cryptocurrencies to invest in, between three or five, so that you will never be too negatively affected by serious drops in one place or another. More than anything else it is going to be important that you control your emotions as thoroughly as possible and strive to avoid rash decisions when investments are on the line. When you are first getting started it is a good idea to not watch your investments too closely, as they are likely going to be all over the place. Don't forget, the goal to long-term investing is a steady overall upward trend which means a little back and forth is to be expected.

It is also important to remember that cryptocurrencies do not come with the lock-in risk that many other long-term investments do. If you feel that a certain cryptocurrency's time has come, you can quickly and easily exchange it with any other currency you choose, instead of having to go through the hassle of trading in a more traditional fashion during a down market. As such, you may want to think about investing in cryptocurrency as just keeping money in a savings account, but one that has a much higher potential for return on your primary investment.

Conclusion

Thank you for reading, let's hope the book was informative and able to provide you with all of the tools you need to achieve your goals, whatever it is that they may be. Just because you've finished this book doesn't mean there is nothing left to learn on the topic, expanding your horizons is the only way to find the mastery you seek.

This is especially true for the blockchain market as it is a new enough technology as to literally be always changing. Only by making it a habit to become a lifelong learner will you ever truly get a grasp on it that you will be able to use for your advantage. Whatever you do, always keep in mind that the market is heading towards an inevitable saturation point which means however you decide to interact with blockchain technology you need to ensure you end up on the right side of it.

It is extremely likely that you will not see another technology this disruptive in your lifetime, and with so many technology variations and cryptocurrencies all vying for the market at once, all you need to do is be aware of the possibility of success to be able to seek it out and reap all the related rewards. It also means that there are plenty of ways to fail, however, so you are going to really need to do your homework and ensure that you never make a move without taking all of your options into consideration fist. Remember, investing in blockchain technology is investing in the long-term, slow and steady wins the race.

Ethereum: Beginners Bible - How You Can Profit from Trading & Investing in Ethereum - even if you're a complete novice

By Stephen Satoshi

Introduction

Wow, what a year it's been for Ethereum, and the cryptocurrency market as a whole. We've seen a 5000% price rise, passed 500,000 daily transactions, survived a Vitalik Buterin death rumor, and witnessed Ethereum truly arrive on the stage of the general public and cement itself as the number two cryptocurrency on the planet.

After opening the year sitting at a modest $7.98, with the market cap at a now unthinkably low $698 million, Ethereum continued to steadily rise and then saw its price explode by nearly 400% in just a 3 week period between May and June. After a few months of steady fluctuation between $250-$350, another breakout occured in mid-November and all time highs of over $500 were reached. At the time of writing, Ethereum's price sits at a cool $453, with a market cap of $45 billion. The Ethereum network now processes more than twice the amount of daily transactions as the Bitcoin network, despite Bitcoin's much higher notoriety.

It hasn't all been smooth sailing though, a June rumor, believed to have been started on the anonymous internet forum 4chan, claimed that Ethereum's founder Vitalik Buterin had been killed in a car crash. This led to an almost instant drop in market value of over $4 billion, which was recovered within a few short days.

So that begs the question, are we in a bubble? Only time will tell, but as I'll explain later on in this book, Ethereum is arguably the must bubbleproof cryptocurrency on the market itself for a variety of reasons. The main one being the sheer number of developments and potential use cases for the platform beyond just a means of exchanging value. The fundamental infrastructure of Ethereum has the potential to revolutionize the internet, plus how financial audits, and business transactions are conducted. That alone is enough for it to continue strong gains in the short and long term on the road to mass adoption. That's without discussing the other billion dollar industries it could potentially disrupt

It should also noted, that the cryptocurrency market as a whole is still only 20% as big as the tech market during the Dotcom crash ($300 billion vs. $1.75 trillion).

Finally, thank you for purchasing this book. If you enjoy reading it, I'd appreciate it if you left it a review on Amazon.

Thanks,

Stephen

What is Ethereum?

Ethereum was born in 2013 from a core team of 3 individuals: Vitalik Buterin, a Russian-Canadian programmer, Dr. Gavin Wood a British economist and game theory enthusiast, and Canadian entrepreneur Joseph Lubin. The fundamental idea behind Ethereum is that blockchain technology can be useful for things outside of just cryptocurrency. These included asset issuance, crowdfunding, domain registration, gambling, voting and prediction markets among innumerable other uses.

The main issue with blockchain platforms up to this point is that they were only designed to do one specific action, like Bitcoin for example, which only processes and verifies monetary transactions between two parties.

You can think of Ethereum as more like a smartphone. Smartphones are able to handle a variety of different types of application, with just one operating platform. Likewise for developers, if someone creates a smartphone application, then all they have to do is upload it to the app store, and users can download it without needing to buy additional hardware. Applications that run on Ethereum are known as Decentralized Apps (DApps).

What is a smart contract?

One of the fundamental ideas behind Ethereum is the use of self-executing smart contracts. We can think of a smart contract like a digital vending machine. A vending machine is a very basic way to ensure a financial agreement is upheld by two parties. Party a) the user and party b) the machine itself. Using a vending machine that dispenses Coke cans as an example. Let's say the cans cost $1.

- If we put it $1, and a coke comes out - successful transaction, and enforcement of the contract

- If we don't put in $1, and no coke comes out - successful enforcement of the contract

- If we don't put in $1, and a coke comes out - something has gone wrong, the contract hasn't been enforced correctly

In the case of a smart contract, the machine in question is a computer algorithm.

To use another example, you could set up a contract where the title deed of a home is transferred from a seller to a buyer, as soon as the buyer's money is sent to the seller. This transaction would usually require a third party to verify it (and thus incur an extra cost), but using smart contracts, the transaction executes automatically once both sides have upheld their part of the agreement, so a third party is not necessary. The lack of a third party, such as a bank or auditor, has the potential for huge cost savings across a wide variety of industries.

Is Ethereum the same as Bitcoin?

Not really. They are both distributed public blockchain networks, that much is true - but that's pretty much where the similarities end. As previously mentioned, Bitcoin only has a singular function which is a peer-to-peer electronic cash system to handle payments online between two parties. Bitcoin's blockchain is only used to track these payments and determine who owns how many coins.

Ethereum on the other hand is used as a platform for running many different kinds of decentralized applications. Unlike Bitcoin, Ethereum has multiple functions, beyond just functioning as an alternative method for payments. Ethereum tokens (known as

Ether, although the terms are often used interchangeably) are used to process the running of the applications, essentially to "pay" for space on the Ethereum platform. A kind of fuel that is used to run the requested operations of the specific application and the execution of smart contracts.

To use an example of a smart contract versus just a transaction. We can compare Bitcoin to Ethereum.

Bitcoin can process a transaction of 1 Bitcoin (BTC) from Steve to Sarah. We can see how much Steve sent, and how much Sarah received.

What Ethereum can do is set up a contract where Steve will send Sarah 1BTC on a set date in the future, but only on the condition that Sarah has less than 10BTC in her Bitcoin wallet on that date. So if Sarah has more than 10BTC on that date, the contract knows it is should not execute, and transaction will not take place.

Another way you could look at Bitcoin vs. Ethereum is that Bitcoin is version 1.0 of a blockchain use case whereas Ethereum is version 2.0. Others like to use a Netscape vs. Google Chrome analogy.

So is Ethereum a programming language like Javascript or Ruby on Rails?

Again, not really. Ethereum is just a blockchain platform that applications can be built on. You can think of it more like an operating system like Windows or iOS. The apps and smart contracts themselves are programmed in a variety of languages such as Solidity.

How does Ethereum have value?

So if Ethereum isn't purely a cryptocurrency, how does it have value? The answer is that Ethereum tokens (ETH or ether) have value as long as the Ethereum network is up and running. The more programs that are running on the network, the more ETH are needed to keep the network running, and therefore the higher the value of ETH. You can think of this like the total amount of gas needed to run all the cars in the world. By buying Ethereum, you are showing faith in the network and the applications that are running on it.

Who is Vitalik Buterin?

While the identity of Bitcoin's "figurehead" Satoshi Nakamoto has never truly been revealed, and may not even be a single person - Ethereum followers can look firmly towards Vitalik Buterin as the leader for the project.

An unassuming looking 23 year old born in Russian, raised in Canada, with a love of unicorn t-shirts, mismatched socks and decentralization principles, Buterin's first entry to the cryptocurrency world was hearing about Bitcoin from his Father at the tender age of 17. He claims he dismissed the idea of cryptocurrency at first, believing there was no intrinsic value, but after quitting his World of Warcraft obsession, he sought something else to sink his time into.

Naturally, being a teenager and having somewhat of an "us versus them" mentality against large centralized institutions, he reexamined cryptocurrency and eventually began writing for a Bitcoin blog, in which he was paid 5BTC (then worth around $50) for each article. Buterin then went on to co-found Bitcoin Magazine, while studying at the University of Waterloo.

Buterin co-founded Ethereum at the tender age of 19 - with the aim of creating a network that could deliver multiple digital services without the need for a middle man by using smart contracts. This in turn would help regulate and govern the "double spending problem" that cryptocurrencies face.

In Buterin's own words, Ethereum was created to be a "general purpose blockchain", a move that some commentators called "impossibly ambitious", although many in the cryptocurrency space saw the move as revolutionary. A 2014 crowdsale raised 31,000 Bitcoins, which was trading at around $650 during the time, but crashed a few weeks later, leaving Buterin and his team with a much lower dollar value than they had previously anticipated. This didn't deter them and by spring of the following year, the early stages of the Ethereum project were online. Within just a few short years, his vision has already begun to take shape. After co-founders Wood and Lubin left the project, Buterin continued as the sole figurehead of the Ethereum foundation.

On June 25th 2017, Buterin was the subject of a hoax regarding his death, believed to be started on 4chan. The rumor stated that Buterin had died in a fatal car crash and this caused $4 billion to be wiped from Ethereum's value as a number of parties panic sold their ETH. Within 12 hours, Buterin himself responded and proved that he was, in fact, alive.

Today, Buterin continues to be part-programmer, part-figurehead for the Ethereum project, albeit with a much larger team behind him. Dealing with the political and social consequences of running a giant blockchain project, as well as, working behind the scenes to improve the technology at the heart of it.

Challenges Ethereum faces going forward

Ethereum, like Bitcoin is now experiencing more and more of a network effect, and has cemented itself as the number 2 cryptocurrency going forward. It's addition onto popular newbie friendly exchange Coinbase has served as a positive for the mass market looking to get involved with cryptocurrencies. However, there a still a number of challenges Ethereum faces going forward on its path towards mass adoption.

Hacking Incidents

The 2016 DAO hacking incident

"The DAO" was a cryptocurrency that had an ICO in April of 2016, with the intention of providing the market with "smart locks" that essentially let people rent out their assets including cars and housing. Sort of a decentralized AirBNB model.

In the first 15 days of its ICO, The DAO raised over $100 million, and reached over $150 by the end of the funding period, which at the time was the largest amount raised by any ICO to date, and represented roughly 14% of all the ETH tokens on the open market. Although during the sale period, several commentators noted that the code was vulnerable to an attack.

On June 18th, a hacker moved 3.6 million ETH (then worth around $50 million) into a clone of the network. 2 days later, in a controversial move, the Ethereum community voted to hard fork the blockchain and restore the funds. This led to the creation of Ethereum Classic (traded as ETC), which maintains itself on the original blockchain.

The incident caused a 33% drop in Ethereum's value overnight. A year later, the thief's identity has still not been brought to light, although Ethereum itself has recovered.

The 2017 Parity wallet deletion incident

One of the stranger Ethereum events of 2017 was the freezing of roughly $200m dollars worth of Ethereum in the digital currency wallet Parity in November. A user managed to trigger an error during a wallet update which led to thousands of ETH being frozen. This error was caused by the user making himself the "owner" of one of Parity's smart contracts and deactivating the contract, which in turn froze the assets inside it.

Due to the way cryptocurrencies work, the only way these funds would be recoverable is to do a "hard fork" of the Ethereum blockchain when a certain fraction of miners refuse to update their ledgers, which would result in new ones being created. Hard forks themselves are risky, and usually have short term damaging affects on consumer confidence.

It should be noted that this was a problem with Parity's smart contracts, and not the Ethereum blockchain itself. There was a small dip in price (<3%) which showed that the market understood that this was a third party error. However, it does serve as a warning to keeping your crypto assets in a centrally controlled third party wallet.

As of the time of writing, total losses from the parity incident are unconfirmed, with most estimates ranging from $150 million to $300m dollars worth of ETH.

Motherboard news summed up the incident with a great analogy "*[The User] was jiggling door handles and when one door opened, they tried to close it and the whole house exploded.*"

With both of these hacking incidents it should be reiterated that the Ethereum network itself was not hacked. All networked systems are vulnerable to various kinds of attacks. The Ethereum network, which supports (depending on the price) around $1bn worth of ether, has not been hacked and is continuously executing many other smart contracts.

Vitalik as a Central Figurehead

Vitalik Buterin himself is another point where Ethereum could face issues going forward. Any central figurehead is going to be largely scrutinized and

Buterin is no different. A comparison can be made to Litecoin, with founder Charlie Lee coming under continued pressure for comments he has made about various cryptocurrencies and the cryptocurrency space in general.

However, Buterin continues to take on the role of developer first and foremost rather than a traditional "frontman" so to speak. The argument could also be made that as the project is still very much in the early stages, a central figurehead is needed. It is likely that once Ethereum reaches more a "finalized" version, Buterin would be expected to move away from a public position.

Scalability

The problem with most larger cryptocurrencies is the problem of scalability. Can their networks handle a huge volume of transactions, without incurring high fees. For example, the average Bitcoin transaction now costs around $4 in network fees. Ethereum on the hand has lower amounts, but will need to keep these low, will still trying to handle a large volume of transactions. Vitalik Buterin outlined a plan at the BeyondBlock conference, for Ethereum to reach "Visa levels" of scalability, without compromising core values such as safety, security and decentralization. To give an example of how ambitious that is, Ethereum processes 15 transactions per second, compared to Visa's 45,000 per second.

Ethereum's solution to the scaling problem in the short term is the launch of the Raiden network. Raiden aims to shift the majority of transactions off of the main Ethereum blockchain by using a technique known as "sharding". This essentially breaks the transaction down into tiny pieces, allowing the pieces to run on different networks, and because the networks are all interlinked - the transaction can process the same way as it were on a single network.

While no specific time frame has been discussed for reaching this so-called "Visa level" - the launch of Raiden and continued updates to the Ethereum network could see much of Ethereum's scalability issues solved within the next 5 years.

Advice on investing in Ethereum and cryptocurrency

Beyond my usual advice of never invest more than you can afford to lose. There are a number of areas your should consider before you invest in Ethereum or any other cryptocurrency.

1.   Market Volatility

Cryptocurrency as a market is extremely volatile when compared to other financial markets such as derivatives and foreign exchange. Swings of 10% either way in a day are not uncommon, and smaller currencies can see their price double in a matter of hours (or in the case of Ethereum, rise 400% in just under 3 weeks). If you are a cautious investor, then cryptocurrency may not be for you, because with the potential for large gains comes an inherently larger risk. One additional note should be that the cryptocurrency market is open 24/7, and price moves can often happen while US or European citizens are asleep, thanks to the large volume of trading that occurs in China and South Korea. That said, Ethereum is one of the more stable cryptocurrencies.

2. Dollar Cost Averaging

Before investing in cryptocurrency, it's wise to do some basic risk management. Traditional investing advice dictates that you should only invest 10% of your overall portfolio in high risk investments, and cryptocurrency definitely checks the box as a high risk investment.

Secondly, to remove your exposure to market volatitlity, you should employ what is known as dollar cost averaging when investing. That means, instead of investing a large lump sum at once, you divide that sum up and invest a little bit at equal time periods.

For example, instead of investing $12,000 all at once, break that $12,000 up and invest $1,000 every month over the course of the year.

The reason for this is that if the price suddenly dips 20% the day after your initial investment, your loss in terms of $ is lower if your use dollar cost averaging. You can then benefit from buying more at this new lower price the next month. So over the course of the year, your average purchase price is usually lower. I would strongly advise you utilize dollar cost averaging when you invest in cryptocurrency, or any financial market.

3. Diversification

If you do decide to invest in cryptocurrency, then Ethereum should by no means be your only holding. It should make up a large chunk of your portfolio, but diversifying is never a bad idea. Bitcoin of course is well worth looking into, as are the other smaller cap coins I discuss later on in this book. Once again, do you own research, and buy on fundamentals rather than hype.

4. Misinformation, fake news and FUD

Because the cryptocurrency market is still in its infancy, there are still very few reliable news sources, and unfortunately a larger number of unreliable ones. There's no bigger proof of this than looking back to the rumors of Vitalik Buterin's death in June 2017, which caused Ethereum's value to drop by $4 billion in just a few short hours.

The flipside of this is that mainstream major outlets do not employ cryptocurrency experts, and often will have traditional stock market analysts try to analyze the cryptocurrency market, which works in a completely different way. As such, there are often misleading headlines, poorly researched news stories, and downright incorrect technical information.

There are also those who intentionally spread misinformation about that cryptocurrency market, which causes Fear, Uncertainty & Doubt, known in the space as "FUD". FUD is different from pointing out legitimate flaws or challenges in cryptocurrency, as the sole intentional is to cause negative price movements, rather than spark actual discussion about the technology.

You should certainly stay informed with the latest Ethereum news, but there are better sources than others. Below are 4 websites that in my opinion offer the best, unbiased cryptocurrency news, without any of the hype or spin that you'll find on other websites.

http://coindesk.com

http://cointelegraph.com

https://coincenter.org - Focuses on cryptocurrency legislation

http://cryptopanic.org - A cryptocurrency news aggregator platform

I would also be wary of paid newsletters or websites that offer cryptocurrency investment advice. While many of these predictions and "tips" have grown in value in 2017, it should be noted that this is one of the biggest bull markets ever seen, so there are a disproportionately high number of winners this year alone. I advise you to do your own research first and foremost, before blindly putting your faith in one of these services.

5. Your reasons for investing

You should ask yourself if you believe in Ethereum, and blockchain technology as a whole, at a technological level before you invest. Blockchain is transforming the landscape of computing, finance and governance as we know it, but that doesn't necessarily mean all of these companies have functional or even useful products that the mass market will gladly adopt.

If you truly believe (as many do, including myself), that Ethereum and blockchain technology is here to stay, and that will correspond in higher prices, then by all means invest your money. However, if your motivations for investing are purely down to the fear of missing out, and the expectation of indefinite continuous price rises, then you may be better off keeping your money elsewhere.

6. Don't day trade unless you know what you're doing, and have previous day trading experience

While day trading may seem like the quickest way to make a lot of money, it's also the quickest way to lose a lot of money if you don't know what you're doing. If you've never day traded before, I would *not* recommend you start with something as volatile as cryptocurrency. Remember, the vast majority of day traders lose money.

Is Mining Ethereum worth it?

In one of my other books, *Bitcoin: Beginners Bible*, I outlined why I believed mining Bitcoins was a bad idea for the average person. I believe the same general advice is true for Ethereum, but for slightly different reasons.

While ASICs (powerful computer that are only built to perform one task, in this case cryptocurrency mining) are not available for Ethereum, which makes the network rewards higher for smaller miners, the electricity costs of mining in the Western world now offset these rewards. The Ethereum block reward was recently decreased from 5ETH per block to 3ETH per block. So once again, you will need a dedicated mining machine to make any sort of significant mining gains.

These dedicated machines require large capital investment, for example, the NVidia GTX1070, currently considered the best mining GPU available, costs $500, and for an efficient mining rig you'll need 6 of these. That's not even considering the other computer parts you'll require.

As a rough estimate for a US citizen mining at home, it would take 2 years for you to recoup your investment, and that is assuming mining rewards stay the same throughout those two years.

The opportunity cost of your investment is also money you could have just invested in Ethereum itself. For example, if you'd spent $5,000 on a mining rig at the start of the year, you'd have recouped roughly half of your initial investment by November. Whereas if you had invested that $5,000 in Ethereum tokens, your returns would be roughly $280,000.

There are other cryptocurrencies that are still profitable to mine at home, Monero being the main one as of November 2017, but as for Ethereum, you are better off putting your resources into direct investments.

How to buy Ethereum in less than 15 minutes

Okay, so you've done your reading and you're ready to jump into the world of cryptocurrency and buy some Ethereum of your very own. First of all, congratulations and welcome to the club. Now, let's get you some Ethereum.

Coinbase

Coinbase represents the most simple way to buy Ethereum for those living in the US, Canada, the UK and Australia, in exchange for your local fiat currency. Based out of the US and regulated by the SEC, Coinbase is undoubtedly the most trustworthy cryptocurrency exchange out there today. Rates are competitive with the other major cryptocurrency exchanges, and the verification requirements are solid without being a hassle.

Currently Coinbase supports both wire transfers and purchases by debit and credit card. Once you signup for a Coinbase account and verify your ID, you can buy Ethereum, along with Bitcoin and Litecoin, instantly with your debit or credit card.

You can also store your cryptocurrency in Coinbase's vault system. If you do this, you will have to pass 2 factor authentication in order to spend it. This is one step more secure than simply leaving it on the exchange, but still is not as secure as offline storage option such as MyEtherWallet.

Another advantage of Coinbase is that they have a fully functional mobile app that allows the buying and selling of cryptocurrency on the go.

Now, as a special bonus to you - if you sign up for Coinbase using this link, you will receive $10 worth of free Bitcoin after your first purchase of more than $100 worth of Bitcoin, Ethereum or Litecoin.

http://bit.ly/10dollarbtc

Once you have purchased your Ethereum, there are a number of other exchanges I recommend if you want to trade Ethereum, many smaller cap cryptocurrencies do not allow for direct exchanges with fiat currency like USD, so you'll have to buy Bitcoin or Ethereum from Coinbase first, then exchange that for the other cryptocurrencies.

Poloniex

With more than 100 different cryptocurrencies available and data analysis for advanced traders, Poloniex is arguably the most comprehensive exchange on the market. Low trading fees (between 0.1 and 0.25%) are another plus, which makes this is a great place to trade your Bitcoin or Ethereum into other cryptocurrencies. The big drawback of Poloniex is that it does not allow fiat currency deposits, so you will have to make your initial Bitcoin or Ethereum purchases on Coinbase.

EtherDelta

EtherDelta is especially useful for buying and selling ERC20 in exchange for Ethereum. While not the most aesthetically pleasing website to look at, EtherDelta employs Ethereum smart contracts to function as a decentralized Ethereum exchange. Currently there are over 100 different token available for purchase.

Exchanges I do not recommend

Kraken

I used to recommend Kraken as a solid Coinbase alternative, however their decreasing levels of customer support and increased downtime over the past 6 months has led me stop recommend them.

BitStamp

Questionable customer service decisions. One user reported a termination on an account with more than 60,000 EUR worth of ETH and XRP inside, but did not receive the funds back from Bitstamp, either in cryptocurrency or in fiat. While this issue, and others like it, are still ongoing, I cannot recommend the exchange.

Where to store your

Ethereum - setting up your

Ethereum wallet

It is advisable that you do not keep any Ethereum (or any cryptocurrency for that matter), on a centralized exchange. The reason for this is that any cryptocurrency you store on an exchange is that directly controlled by you. This makes it vulnerable to attacks from third parties, and hacking incidents like the Mt. Gox hack of 2014.

Setting up Mist Wallet

Mist wallet is a simple way to store your Ethereum on your own personal computer rather than on a centralized exchange. This is more secure than an exchange, but for maximum security online storage (such as MyEtherWallet or a hardware wallet) is still recommended.

1. Go to https://github.com/ethereum/mist/releases and download the latest version for either PC, Mac or Linux

2. Install the wallet on your computer

3. Once installed click on "USE THE TEST NETWORK" and set your password. Use a unique password that you DO NOT use for any other website

4. Now you'll be able to see the wallets page and you balance should read 0.00ETH

5. Click on "Main account" - you will see your unique wallet address here, this will be 40 characters longer and will start start with 0x. If you share this address with someone, they will be able to send you Ether.

6. You can also send ETH from your account to any other ETH wallet address using Mist. You'll need your password to do so. When you do this you will see a confirmation number, you can check the transaction has processed correctly by copying this to http://testnet.etherscan.io/

How to set up an offline wallet with MyEtherWallet

All the coins in this book are based on the Ethereum blockchain, and therefore use ERC20 tokens. Therefore, these tokens can be stored in Ethereum wallets like regular ETH. Wallets can be daunting to set up at first, so I recommend you use something simple to get started, the most convenient of these is MyEtherWallet.

Step-by-Step guide to setting up MyEtherWallet

13. Go to https://www.myetherwallet.com/

14. Enter a strong but easy to remember password. Do not forget it.

15. This encrypts (protects) your private key. It does not generate your private key. This password alone will not be enough to access your coins.

16. Click the "Generate Wallet" button.

17. Download your Keystore/UTC file & save this file to a USB drive.

18. This is the encrypted version of your private key. You need your password to access it. It is safer than your unencrypted private key but you must have your password to access it in the future.

19. Read the warning. If you understand it, click the "I understand. Continue" button.

20. Print your paper wallet backup and/or carefully hand-write the private key on a piece of paper.

21. If you are writing it, I recommend you write it 2 or 3 times. This decreases the chance your messy handwriting will prevent you from accessing your wallet later.

22. Copy & paste your address into a text document somewhere.

23. Search your address on https://etherscan.io/ Bookmark this page as this is how you can view your balance at any time

24. Send a small amount of any coin from your previous wallet or exchange to your new wallet - just to ensure you have everything correct

Hardware Wallets

- Another safe, offline solution is to use a hardware wallet. The most popular of these being Trezor and Nano S. Both of these cost around $100, but represent a convenient, yet safe way to store your cryptocurrency.

To get your own Trezor wallet go to

http://bit.ly/GetTrezorWallet

Cryptocurrencies built using Ethereum blockchain technology

It' not just Ethereum that relies on Ethereum technology. There are many other cryptocurrencies that use the same blockchain for specific use cases.

It may surprise you to know that there are currently **over 5000 ERC20 tokens.** One of the many positives of Ethereum technology is that it has made token creation extremely accessible, and as such the number of new tokens on the market has increased exponentially in the past 18 months.

Now obviously some are better than others, and in this section we'll examine a few of the more interesting ones and their potential use cases moving forward. Alongside each currency I've included its price and market cap at the time of writing, as well as, which cryptocurrency exchanges you can purchase it from and information about where to store it.

Augur (REP)

Price at Time of Writing - $20.19

Market Cap at Time of Writing - $219,749,200

Available on:

Fiat: Kraken

BTC: Poloniex, Bittrex, Liqui

Where to Store: Augur is an ERC20 token so can be stored in MyEtherWallet

Augur is a prediction market platform that uses Ethereum smart contracts to ensure correct payouts for correct predictions. Users can user it to predict real world events, and are rewarded if they are correct.

For example, you can predict the outcome of a Presidential election, a sporting event like the NBA finals or the winners of an Oscar award. Where Augur differs from a traditional gambling platform, is that instead of laying down a flat fee on an outcome at certain betting odds - you actually buy shares in an event.

For example, if you think Hillary Election would be elected President, and the market gives that a 50% chance, you essentially buy 50% of the shares of that outcome. If the market then moves, the odds become better than even, say 60%, your 50% share is now worth more than when you originally bought so you can sell it for a profit, before the event outcome is known.

Prediction markets like this have been proven to be more accurate over time than individuals. This phenomenon is known as "the wisdom of the crowd", or that a group of people is better on average at predicting events than any one person inside that group. This is especially true when those predicting are laying real money down on an event outcome.

Where Augur really shines though is that anyone can create their own prediction market. A small fee is required (to provide initial funding), and in return the creator of the market receives a percentage of all trading fees from that particular market. This decentralized approach is one that allows much lower fees than traditional, non-blockchain based prediction platforms.

This decentralization also adds an additional element of security, as the market cannot be subject of the manipulation of an individual, or small group of individuals like centralized markets. For example, someone has to actually report whether the event occured or not e.g. whether Clinton or Trump became

President. With a centralized market, this can be subject to lies or outright corruption. With Augur, because each market has hundreds or even thousands of reporters, and the reports are publicly available for every to see, the correct result is always ensured. The Ethereum smart contracts also ensure regular, on-time payments for the correct amount - free from human error

Currently, a beta version of the platform is in development. This beta version will use virtual money only. This is done to test the coding of the smart contracts, and in case anything does go wrong in the beta stages, no one's funds are lost. The beta version of the AUGUR is also currently limited to markets with binary or "yes/no" outcomes, although there are plans to expand on this in the final version of the platform. The release date is currently scheduled for Q1 2018, although no formal release date has been announced yet.

Augur's tokens are known as reputation tokens or REP. 11 million were denominated during the ICO period, and this supply is designed to be fixed, so none can be mined. Those holding REP, and with a status set to "active" on the platform, will be expected to participate in the markets. If reporters do not report accurate results, they will be docked REP, which again ensures the legitimacy of the platform.

The team currently provides bi-weekly updates on their blog, part of these updates include offering REP in return for beta testers solving bugs in the code. Garnering community involvement like this has been hugely beneficial for other cryptocurrencies in the past.

Augur's price in the short term is likely to depend on how successful the launch of their beta platform is.

Longer term, mass adoption versus traditional prediction markets is the main factor - will the masses see a blockchain solution as necessary in this particular use case?

TenX (PAY)

Price at Time of Writing - $2.26

Market Cap at Time of Writing - $209,278,662

Available on:

Fiat: Kraken

BTC: Bit-Z, Bittrex, Liqui

ETH: Bittrex, Liqui, EtherDelta

Where to store: Augur is an ERC20 token so can be stored in MyEtherWallet

Based out of Singapore, summarizing TenX can be best done with this quote from Inc. Magazine about the project

"TenX has figured out how to solve one of the biggest problems for people that are involved in cryptocurrency – actually spending the currency."

To elaborate, the TenX project is a platform that allows blockchain assets to be spent by individual users in the real world. One of the main issues with the growth of the cryptocurrency market as a whole, is with the constant additions of new token, how do uses actually spend them - without having to convert them back to Bitcoin or Ethereum, and then in some cases, back to fiat currency. The problem here lies with the transaction fees involved for these conversions, because they can add up fast, especially if you wish to carry out multiple transaction per day.

TenX plans to solve this by offering a debit card, that allows users to spend their cryptocurrencies at any regular point of sale system, this card is linked to a mobile wallet stored on their smartphone. Users can even spend their crypto assets directly via their smartphones at selected locations. Even today in the early stages of the project, the card is usable in over 200 countries, at over 36 million points of sale.

The key point to note here is that the cryptocurrencies stored in the TenX wallet are not converted to fiat currency until they are spent. This conversion then happens in real time. This also allows up to real-time currency conversions and the best possible foreign exchange rates and the lowest transaction fees.

The product has already completed a closed beta testing phase, with over 1,000 users testing the app in the real world, the total transaction volume during the beta phase was over $100,000. The beta tested version supported Bitcoin only, but the final platform aims to support Ethereum, along with ERC20 tokens and Dash in the short term, with support for additional cryptocurrencies planned in the long term. A public beta version is scheduled for release in Q4 2017, with a fully operational platform scheduled for Q2 2018.

Users in EU countries, along with select other European countries can now order TenX debit cards direct from the TenX website itself. There are plans to roll out the service in other countries, including the USA, in the coming months. With any payment platform like this, there are a number of compliance issues that have to be resolved - especially one that wishes to use the VISA debit card standard like TenX

There have been some issues however, with unprecedented demand for the cards themselves, which has in-turn caused a large backlog of orders. Currently the backlog stands at around 3 months, which is a major issue that will have to be resolved if the platform is going to have any sort of wider adoption.

TenX tokens (known as PAY) are used to incentivize usage of the platform. Users earn a 0.1% reward every time they use the app to spend their crypto assets, this reward is denominated in PAY. Currently this reward is distributed on a monthly basis, although there are plans to make this distribution as frequently as every hour in the future.

Holders of PAY tokens also receive a 0.5% reward based on the total transaction volume of the platform for the month. This reward is then multiplied by the number of PAY tokens each user has, so the more tokens one holds, the higher their reward.

During the ICO period, 51% of the total amount of PAY tokens were distributed to investors, with an additional 29% held back for further development of the platform. The team's long-term goal is to make

80% of the tokens available to the public, with the rest held by the founders and early developers.

One thing I particularly like about the TenX project is the team's commitment to wider cryptocurrency education through their YouTube channel. Cryptocurrency is still very much in the infant stages of its lifecycle, and any educational resources aimed at the general public can be looked at in a positive light.

The success of TenX going forward will depends on a number of factors. The first is competition, they aren't the only "cryptocurrency debit card" player in town. Monaco could be considered their main rival at this stage, although I'm sure that other similar projects will pop up in the near future. The second is the speed at which they can support various currencies in the app and card itself. Support for the big 3 cryptocurrencies (Bitcoin, Ethereum and Litecoin) would be huge for short term gains, and support for all ERC20 tokens would also be a positive as we move beyond 2018.

Storj (STORJ)

Price at Time of Writing - $0.678

Market Cap at Time of Writing - $70,896,782

Available on:

BTC: Binance, Bittrex, Poloniex

ETH: Binance, Bittrex, Liqui, Gate.io

Where to store: Storj is an ERC20 token so can be stored in MyEtherWallet

Storj (pronounced: storage) plans to take on the multi million dollar cloud storage industry with a decentralized blockchain solution. The team estimates that with a decentralized solution rather than a traditional model, cloud storage can be up to 10x faster and 50% less expensive.

Traditional cloud storage like say Dropbox, involves users uploading their files to a single, central server. Whereas with a decentralized model, these files are first encrypted to ensure their security, and then globally distributed across a set of storage nodes using blockchain technology.

The major problem that traditional centralized cloud storage companies face is that because there is one point of failure for the network, the network can suffer periodic downtime. Using a decentralized model, with the data effectively being stored in thousands of different locations, the network will not suffer from the downtime issues.

The other main issue that centralized storage faces is the security of the data itself. Once again, because there is a single point of entry to the server, there is also a single point of failure. This means no matter how good the encryption is, hackers could eventually get a hold of data. With a decentralized model, because the files are spread across thousands of different nodes

Another innovative function is the ability for users to effective rent out their unused hard drive space to users on the Storj network. This is known as Storj Share and users, known as "farmers" will be paid for their space in Storj tokens.

The Storj network is currently up and running, with a transparent pricing model, based only on what you use. Storage costs $0.015 per GB, per month with no minimum usage. So 100GB of storage would cost $1.50 per month. The platform has already attracted 25,000 users along with 19,000 farmers. An enterprise level model is also up and running, with an agreement already signed with a Fortune 500 company back in 2016.

One area that Storj may face trouble with is the hosting of illegal content via their service. The decentralized and encrypted nature of the platform makes it impossible to know exactly what kind of files are being hosted. The Storj team recognize this and are putting their faith in the userbase to use the service "within society's legal and ethical norms" and the ability for users to "graylist" certain content.

For example, those offering storage space could decide they do not want any pornographic material hosted using their space. You could argue that this is a centralized measure, but it should be noted that this only affects files hosted publicly, those hosted privately will be unaffected. Graylists will also be a strictly optional, opt-in required feature.

The coin has already received its fair share of support from big names in the Ethereum blockchain space, including Vitalik Buterin himself. This combined with a working product, make it an intriguing proposition as we move into 2018 and beyond.

Storj has also targeted an expansion into China to compete in their often difficult to penetrate cloud storage market. Regulations requiring overseas providers to partner with local companies caused Amazon to eventually sell $300m worth of its Chinese cloud storage assets to its local partner. Storj has partnered with Shanghai based startup Genaro in its own bid to expand into the large Chinese market.

Monaco (MCO)

Price at Time of Writing - $6.48

Market Cap at Time of Writing - $63,811,823

Available on:

BTC: Bittrex, Binance, Liqui

ETH: Bittrex, Binance, Liqui

Where to store: Monaco is an ERC20 token so can be stored in MyEtherWallet

Based out of Switzerland, Monaco aims to bridge fiat and cryptocurrency with an all-in-one debit card and mobile wallet app. The project should be looked at slightly differently to other cryptocurrency projects, as this one isn't strictly about cryptocurrency itself. You can look at Monaco more like a fintech project utilizing the cryptocurrency space.

Using their fair usage model, users won't be charged monthly or annual fees for holding the card. Monaco currently users VISA debit cards and the VISA payment platform so has access to over 40 million merchants worldwide. The project received official partnership with VISA in September 2017 and Monaco is now registered under the VISA Program Manager initiative which allows them further say in areas such as cashback rewards for their clients.

There are numerous features such as the card always using the local currency. So if you're someone who travels a lot, you'll have access to the official inter-bank exchange rate, rather than the consumer rate which is often 2-3% higher. Anyone who travels frequently will be able to understand that these savings add up quickly. Research has demonstrations this could represent savings of between $60-80 per $1000 spent.

The card also offers cryptocurrency cashback up to 2% with all purchases. Cashback cards are nothing new and have been around for decades, but Monaco represents the first one in the cryptocurrency space. The cashback will be in the form of Monaco (MCO) tokens. The cashback program is planned to offer higher rewards (of up to 10%) once wider adoption occurs.

The Monaco app can also be used to send instant payments to your friends and family, this can be done in multiple currencies including Bitcoin and Ethereum. On average, this will save 4% for international currency conversions when compared to regular banks.

Rollout of Monaco cards continues to rely on local compliance checks. The first cards will be shipped to those in Singapore after passing national governance tests in late October 2017. Over 17,000 cards have already been reserved and users can reserve their own by downloading the Monaco app for either Android or iOS. Demand is expected to be high and the Monaco team have already ordered over 500,000 physical cards.

Like most early stage projects, it hasn't been all smooth sailing for Monaco. A post-ICO price peak of $24 has been followed by steady declines throughout the year. This is partly due to initial ICO hype wearing off (pretty much every 2017 ICO has suffered from this), the other part is due to an issue with the smart contract mechanism in place. The original smart contract had to be re-worked in order to gain SEC compliance

Growth of Monaco is based firmly on passing compliance protocols across various markets. For example, their roadmap targets US approval within the first half of 2018, with European approval expected before then. Before then, news of Monaco being listed on more exchanges is what the community is looking for.

The team have experience in the payments space, for example the CFO is a former executive at MasterCard and they have advisers with previous experience at Visa and AWS.

The issue with Monaco going forward is that there is *a lot* of competition in the cryptocurrency debit card payments space already. I mentioned TenX earlier in this book, a project with similar intentions and there are other projects such as the UK based LBX along with TokenCard and Exscudo. There's no reason that a few of these cannot co-exist, but it will gradually be harder and harder to find a USP within the industry.

Selling points like better exchange rates and cashback are effectively a race to the bottom and there may have to be significant additions to the Monaco project for it to be the consensus leader in the space. We are still in the very early days of cryptocurrency though, and once the card itself rolls out - there are sure to be interesting developments both as a technology, and as a financial asset. Monaco is definitely one to watch as we enter 2018, with potential industry wide ramifications going into 2019 and beyond.

Aragon (ANT)

Price at Time of Writing - $1.67

Market Cap at Time of Writing - $57,369,782

Available on:

BTC: Bittrex, Liqui

ETH: Bittrex, Liqui

Where to Store: Aragon is an ERC20 token so can be stored in MyEtherWallet

Aragon aims to use Ethereum blockchain technology to remove the needs for unnecessary intermediaries in the business world. This concept of Decentralized Autonomous Organizations (DAOs) is a common one in the blockchain space. The number of third parties needed to create and maintain a company leads to market inefficiencies, lower profits, and hampers the ability of that company to provide the best possible product or service for its customers.

The aim of Aragon is to provide everything a person needs to run their organization. This includes services such as payroll, accounting and governance. This leads to greater company transparency, greater cost efficiency and the ability to safely alter a contract without the mound of excess paperwork that comes with traditional contracts.

The ease at which users can perform usually complex tasks like issuing company shares is a huge bonus for small organizations. The fact that all this is transparent as well acts as a built in fraud prevention system. This also applies to raising capital, using Aragon's stock sale voting, it has never been easier for companies to access the capital they require to run their business. Running all this on a publicly accessible blockchain makes budgeting, dividend sharing and general accounting practices incredibly simple.

The Aragon team is headed up by Luis Cuende, who has had a storied history in the blockchain space. Named Europe's best young programmer in 2011 and elected to the Forbes 30 Under 30 list - he previously worked on Blockchain startup Stampery

The test currently has an alpha product available, and 3,000 organizations have been built using the test network. A public beta version is currently scheduled for February 2018.

The main hurdles to overcome for Aragon going forward will be the adoption and trust from wider public, especially with regards to issues like contracts and arbitration. Any bugs in the network regarding this will need to be ironed out before a public release of the Aragon network. However, with 3,000 DAOs already on the testnet, this phase of the project continues to shine positive light on Aragon both as a vision, and as a legitimate platform going forward.

There are similar projects in the works, which isn't necessarily a bad thing as it shows that the general demand is there. Colony is another project that is more focused on the day to day operations of a company and could eventually be used as a module within the Aragon network as Aragon supports third party modules.

District0x (DNT)

Price at Time of Writing - $0.039

Market Cap at Time of Writing - $23,255,100

Available on:

BTC: Binance, Bittrex, Liqui

ETH: Binance, Liqui, Mercatox

Where to store:

District0x is currently an ERC20 token and can be stored on My Ether Wallet. You can view how to add DNT as a custom token on https://etherscan.io/token/district0x

District0x has the goal of breaking the internet down into smaller, more manageable pieces. If you've ever seen the movie The Hunger Games, you'll remember each district was focused on a single task: District 7 was the lumber district, District 8 focused on textile production, District 9 with grain etc.

District0x plans to do the same thing with the blockchain technology and Decentralized Autonomous Organizations (DAO). Each district will have its own payment and invoicing system, along with complete self governance. The venture will use the Ethereum blockchain to run smart contracts.

What District0x has done to make to the process user friendly, is combine different necessary (like smart contracts and payment processing) elements into a package, so it's not essential for users to completely understand the technology behind the platform. You can think of this as similar to how Wordpress works for web development. At the core of every district is the ability to operate a market or a bulletin board application.

Currently, there are over 100 district ideas in play. Theoretically, it would allow an individual such as you or me to implement their own version of AirBNB, Craigslist or Uber, without having to go through a middleman like the current system has to. This in turn reduces transaction fees and makes the overall cost lower for all parties involved. There are no fees to create districts, which makes them available to everyone. Currently, refundable deposits are required to put forward a district proposal, once the district passes quality control checks (ensuring the district is not there for malicious intent), the deposit is refunded to the district creator.

One such idea already running is Ethlance, an online freelancing platform similar to Upwork or Fiverr, but without the large transaction fees. Interestingly enough, the District0x team has actually hired developers via Ethlance to help them execute the project.

Another promising proposal is ShipIt, which focuses on the multi-billion dollar shipping industry. The idea is to create a decentralized maritime logistics platform. The sheer number of transactions in this industry alone (trucking, forwarding, warehousing etc.) make this a perfect foil for a blockchain solution.

The framework is in place, however the team needs to do more to gather traction, plus a larger user base to utilize their own districts. The current team is small, with just 10 members, plus an additional adviser, but there will certainly be additions in the future as the project continues to grow. Progress reports are frequent and developments are regular posted on GitHub.

One interesting approach the District0x team are employing is creating a free "education portal" to inform the wider public about the platform, and the real world functionality of districts. They are doing this are they believe the current limiting factor is a general ignorance of the potential of the platform. The portal is scheduled for rollout in Q4 2017.

District0x tokens (DNT) can be used to fund project and stake voting rights in different districts, the more tokens one has, the greater of a say they have. The one issue here is a possible abuse of a "pay to play" system.

The decentralized element of District0x means there is no single point of failure, for example there is no single server that all of the individual districts run from. This ensures that targeted hacking attacks cannot take down the entire network.

Supply wise, there are 600 million DNT available, with a total projected supply of 1 billion. It should be noted that in the white paper, the District0x team does reserve the right to add additional coins to the total supply, however this is contingent on the exchange rate between ETH/USD. For example, if ETH's value declines significantly vs. USD, the team can add additional coins to account for this fluctuation. This isn't necessarily something to be concerned about (financial hedging occurs all the time in fiat markets), but it's definitely something worth nothing.

Listing on larger exchanges will help spike the price in the short term. The team are in ongoing discussions with large exchange Bittrex, and a listing on there could easily see price rises of 100%. Long term prices will be largely determined by the number of popular districts that are set up using the platform. The next

two planned district launches are Name Bazaar and
Meme Factory.

Request Network (REQ)

Price at Time of Writing - $0.066

Market Cap at Time of Writing - $42,266,398

Available on:

BTC: Binance, Liqui

ETH: Binance, KuCoin, EtherDelta

Where to store: REQ is an ERC20 token so can be stored in MyEtherWallet

Request Network aims to become a decentralized payment network allowing both businesses and individuals to request money from anyone. The project aims to bring blockchain technology into the payment provider space, and act as competition to PayPal and Stripe. Request has already received industry plaudits as well as investment from US based startup investment group YCombinator.

Current centralized payment providers and networks take a commission of between 1.5% and 6% per transaction depending on the platform and the type of payment. Request Network aims to lower this fee to as little as 0.05% per transaction, with an average fee of 0.2% per transaction. This represents huge savings to the consumer and the merchant. Request also allows payment in cryptocurrency as well as fiat currency.

By utilizing Ethereum technology, all payments requested and made will be available on a public ledger for anyone to see. This level of transparency lowers the degree of fraudulent payments and fraudulent refund requests that currently plague traditional networks like PayPal and Stripe. This also has residual effects for areas like time sensitive money back guarantees or warranties for items.

Another advantage Request has versus traditional platforms is the transparency leads to lowering auditing costs. For example, in 2014 online Microsoft paid Deloitte over $45 million in auditing fees, and Bank of America paid over $100 million. With Request's public blockchain ledger, audits would effectively be carried out in real time and would represent a far less expensive option than hiring a third party to manual check that the transactions are valid.

Request Network is actually part of the 3,000 companies that are built on the Aragon testnet, which shows the interaction between blockchain projects. Request has also partnered with another blockchain project, Kyber, to improve the automatic currency conversion element of the platform. The Kyber partnership has great real world use potential as the merchant can specify payment in any cryptocurrency of their choosing, and the payee can still pay with their preferred cryptocurrency.

Request also recently introduced continuous payments, which allows users to be paid by the hour (and in theory, by the second). This is an ideal model for contractors or freelancers who work on an hourly basis rather than per project.

The team continues to deliver on the roadmap, with the latest update, known as "Colossus" being delivered ahead of schedule in Q4 2017 rather than the initially anticipated Q1 2018. Q1 2018 will see the "Great Wall" update, with a launch of Request Network on the Ethereum main net for the first time. The Great Wall update is of particular interest as this is when the "Pay with Request" button will be available to those who want to use it alongside traditional methods like "Pay with credit card" and "Pay with PayPal"

The payments sector is huge, and PayPal alone has an annual revenue of over $10 billion. If Request Network can capture even a small fraction of this, then there is potential for enormous growth. Alongside massive opportunity does come a certain amount of competition though, OmiseGO being the most well known one in the cryptocurrency space. There are also Populous and MetalPay, both of which have similar visions to Request.

A Low-Risk (But Still Highly Profitable) Way to Invest in Cryptocurrencies

For those of you familiar with traditional investments, then you'll likely to be aware of Exchange Traded Funds or ETFs. For those unfamiliar, and ETF is a security that trades like a regular stock, but instead of buying shares in one company, you are buying an aggregate of many companies. ETFs have an inherent advantage over single stocks in that by diversifying your risk over many companies, you are less likely to see sudden drops in price.

Based out of Slovenia, and active since November 2016, Fintech start-up Iconomi is currently running a blockchain based digital asset management platform using Ethereum technology. Known as Digital Asset

Arrays (DAA), these are similar to ETFs and Index funds, as you are buying an aggregate of multiple cryptocurrencies instead of just one or two. Initial investments can be made with ETH or BTC, although there are plans to support fiat deposits in the coming months.

Their BLX blockchain index is the first passively managed array of digital assets, compromising of over 20 different cryptocurrencies, with the highest weight being in Bitcoin and Ethereum. The portfolio is re-balanced on a monthly basis, and different cryptocurrencies are added and removed based on performance. What's more is the BLX has currently outperformed both Ethereum and Litecoin over the past 6 months. There is also a more conservative fund which is composed of 60% Bitcoin, 20% Ethereum as well as 4 other ERC20 tokens. The fund have a 2-3% annual management fee, plus a 0.5% exit fee.

This could well be a good option if you're looking to invest in a multitude of cryptocurrencies, but don't want to deal with the hassle of signing up for multiple exchanges, and keeping track of various wallets. Iconomi currently offers 15 different DAAs, ranging from conservative, heavily Bitcoin based ones, to more risky ones featuring a multitude of smaller cap cryptocurrencies. Of course, like any investment, there are inherent risks involved, but if you're a more risk averse investor, who still wants to be a part of the cryptocurrency market, Iconomi is worth checking out.

Determinants of Cryptocurrency Growth Patterns in 2018 and Beyond

Coinbase

Regardless of your personal opinions on Coinbase as a cryptocurrency exchange, it still functions as the vast majority of user's first entry into the cryptocurrency market. It's accessibility and the ability to make purchases via debit and credit card means it's ideal as a "my first cryptocurrency exchange". Currently Coinbase allows the buying and selling of Bitcoin, Ethereum and Litecoin in exchange for fiat. However in November 2017, Coinbase announced that it would list ERC20 tokens in 2018, and any of the ERC20 below tokens being listed on Coinbase is sure to have a positive effect on price going forward. This also applies to other major exchanges such as Bitfinex and Bittrex, but Coinbase is the milestone here.

Market adoption

The later half of 2017 alone saw the cryptocurrency marketcap more than double to over $300 billion at the time of writing, and we are still very much in the infancy of cryptocurrency. Further investment by new players and a constant influx of new money into the market leads to bullish conditions. According to Forbes magazine, less than 0.5% of the world currently owns any form of cryptocurrency (and the vast majority of this will be Bitcoin).

We could look at this as a similar situation when the technology boom was in 1994, where email was the biggest use case, way before today's social media, video streaming, and online retail services. One could look at Bitcoin as the email of the cryptocurrency market. How does this relate to Ethereum? Well, in Ethereum's case, the vast majority of DApps aren't close to any sort of mass adoption, and it will likely be years before the market has matured.

Regulation

Regulation in various forms can have both positive and negative effects for the market as a whole. Ethereum itself was hit hard when headlines of "China bans ICOs" hit the front pages in late September. However, the news turned out to be temporary and the entire market recovered and surged in October and November. Large scale regulation in the US, China or Russia would indeed have a negative impact on both price and the technology future of Ethereum based projects.

Neo

Neo is the cryptocurrency project most similar to Ethereum in terms of being a platform that other blockchain companies can build on top of. Ethereum has a much wider adoption currently, but Neo is based out of China, and following on from the above point - Chinese government regulation in favor of a "domestic coin" could hurt Ethereum's adoption potential in the Chinese market. For example, an announcement that all Chinese ICOs must be built using Neo is plausible, and as China represents a large part of the cryptocurrency market, this will in turn have a negative effect on Ethereum. That being said, the above is an extreme scenario, and there is no reason that Ethereum and Neo cannot co-exist.

Futures Market & Institutional Investing

Institutional investors will play a big part in the growth of Ethereum as a tradable asset, and the release of an Ethereum futures market, where traders can bet the future price of Ethereum, will signify that it is maturing. As of yet, only Bitcoin futures can be traded, but as Ethereum matures more as an asset, there is no doubt that a similar market for trading ETH will emerge.

Moving to Proof of Stake

One of the largest technological challenges surrounding Ethereum is the move from a Proof of Work (PoW) mining algorithm to a more environmentally friendly Proof of Stake (PoS) one. The original PoW method is similar to the one used by Bitcoin, in that computers solve cryptographic puzzles (or complex mathematical equations) in order to validate a transaction and create a block. This method requires increasing amounts of computing power to mine cryptocurrency, and can leads to issues such as the vast majority of the mining power being concentrated in the hands of just a few miners (for example, someone running a large scale mining operation). It is this kind of centralization that Ethereum seeks to avoid. There is also the issue of electricity use, both Ethereum and Bitcoin are currently estimated to use over $1 million worth of electricity *per day* in their mining process, which is more electricity than a moderately sized country than Ireland or Denmark.

A PoS mining algorithm differs because it allows holders of ETH to deposit or "stake" their coins in order to validate the next block. The public blockchain tracks who holds ETH, and how much of it they have staked. Therefore, you don't need expensive hardware to participate in the mining process. Mining rewards are proportional to how much you have staked, so someone staking 10 ETH would get 10x the rewards of someone staking 1 ETH. PoS also has the advantage of shortening network transaction times, and making them more consistent. So instead of an average transaction time of 15 per second, the 15 transactions confirmed every second, like clockwork. PoS also allows ETH to be used as an asset and could be looked at like a savings account, because if you staked your ETH on the a network, you would essentially receive interest from mining rewards.

Ethereum's initial move will be to a Hybrid PoW/PoS algorithm in the "Casper" update to the platform. At the time of writing, the Casper update is live on the Ethereum TestNet, so the code isn't finalized but it can be tested for security and safety issues.

A full move to PoS is scheduled in Q1/Q2 2018 in the "Metropolis" update. A smooth transition to PoS will leads to a fairer Ethereum mining ecosystem in the long run, but like any big transition of this kind, there are challenges in the execution. Naturally, any safety or security breaches will lead to negative results for Ethereum, as will technical issues such as users not being able to stake their ETH. As the technology is still very much in it infant stages, these are the kinds of areas that we must be extra cautious of when considered investing.

Adoption in Asia

In June of 2017, South Korea overtook the US and China as the largest Ethereum market in terms of daily trading volume. Roughly $200 million of Ethereum is traded everyday on BitHumb, Korea's largest cryptocurrency exchange. Continued adoption in Asia is part of Ethereum's growth plan for 2018 and beyond, with a Chinese office opening next year, and a growing number of partnerships with Chinese companies in the works.

Conclusion

Ethereum has changed the way we look at financial transactions, auditing and the idea of a middleman. Our previous reliance on banks and other financial institutions has been put into question, and we are now moving forward towards a dcentralized financial world. These multibillion dollar corporations and industries are facing disruption, and actual competition, for the first time in over a century.

For consumers, cross border payments at a near-instant transaction time, and far lower transactions fees are making the global economy smaller and more accessible.

Beyond Ethereum, blockchain technology has an additional laundry list of benefits ranging from transparency in elections to easily accessible medical records between parties.

As a commodity, no other financial asset, cryptocurrency or otherwise has produced better returns for investors over the past 12 months.

For those who believe in Ethereum, and Vitalik Buterin's vision for a better world, long may these returns continue.

I hope you've enjoyed this book and that you're now a little bit more informed about how Ethereum works, and more importantly, how it can work for you. Whether you're planning on investing for the long-term - I wish you the best of luck.

Remember, trade rationally and not emotionally. Never invest more than you can afford to lose, and for the love of God - don't check the charts 15 times a day.

Now, if you're ready to make the next step and get involved in the market. I have a small gift for you.

If you sign up for Coinbase using this link, you will receive $10 worth of free Bitcoin after your first purchase of more than $100 worth of cryptocurrency.

http://bit.ly/10dollarbtc

Finally, if you've enjoyed this book I'd really appreciate it if you left a review on Amazon.

Other Books by Stephen Satoshi

All available to purchase on Amazon

Cryptocurrency: Beginners Bible *(also available in audio)*

Cryptocurrency: Top 10 Trading Mistakes Newbies Make - And How To Avoid Them

www.ingramcontent.com/pod-product-compliance
Lightning Source LLC
Chambersburg PA
CBHW071316210326
41597CB00015B/1243